the
healthy Jewish
cookbook

Michael van Straten

the
healthy Jewish
cookbook

100 delicious recipes from the Mediterranean to Persia, Asia and the Far East

Recipes by Sally and Michael van Straten

Recipe photography by Jan Baldwin
Location photography by Vanessa Courtier

Kyle Cathie Ltd

This book is dedicated to the memory of Kate, Ada, Sally, Gertie, Minnie, Leah, Harry and Jimmy – the Greenberg brothers and sisters. They are all gone now, as is my father Louis whom they embraced into their family to make up for the loss of his own during the Holocaust of the Second World War. It's also in memory of their husbands and wives and two of my first cousins Linda and Mark. We were a great and happy family for whom food was the cement that bound us all together, communal meals being the 'band aid' that healed arguments and mended rifts. As long as there are children, grandchildren and great-grandchildren who talk about their parents, aunts and uncles and pass on the family recipes from generation to generation, they will always be with us.

First published in Great Britain 2005 by
Kyle Cathie Limited
122 Arlington Road, London NW1 7HP
general.enquiries@kyle-cathie.com
www.kylecathie.com

10 9 8 7 6 5 4 3 2 1

ISBN 1 85626 559 5

Senior editor Muna Reyal
Art direction and design Vanessa Courtier
Recipe photography Jan Baldwin
Location and chapter opener photography Vanessa Courtier
Home economist David Morgan
Styling Róisín Nield
Copyeditor Jamie Ambrose
Editorial assistant Jennifer Wheatley
Production Sha Huxtable and Alice Holloway

A Cataloguing In Publication record for this title is available from the British Library.

Colour reproduction by Chromagraphic
Printed and bound in China by C & C Offset Printing Company Ltd

contents

My mother's healthy kitchen

My mother, Kate, was a wonderful cook – mostly. True, she could boil the life out of any vegetable and happily incinerate any piece of grilled meat and turn pasta into a glutinous mass. But when it came to soups, stews, casseroles, cakes, biscuits or puddings, she was infallible. When she made strudel you could almost see through the paper-thin sheets of dough. She never trusted any butcher enough to buy minced meat and I still remember happy days turning the handle on the old Spong mincer with its interchangeable blades and the mark it always left when it was clamped to the kitchen tabletop, in spite of the folded-up newspaper.

Kate was one of six sisters and two brothers who grew up in the tenement buildings of London's East End when it was the centre of Jewish life. Brothers Harry and Jimmy and four of the sisters, Kate, Ada, Sally and Gertie, were married. The other two, Minnie and Leah, remained single. My aunt Leah was the cleverest one by far, well-read and intellectual, but she was the one who stayed behind to care for my elderly grandparents and then became the universal aunt, travelling from sister to sister whenever help was needed or illness struck. She spent many years living with us and as a small boy I think I was often awful to her but came to love and respect her dearly as I grew a bit more sensible.

All the sisters were great cooks, each with their own specialities, and of course, as happens in all Jewish families, the husbands of the sisters and all their relatives, and the wives of the brothers with all theirs too, together with all their various offspring, became one huge family of *mespucha* – an untranslatable Yiddish word which embraces any relative of any relative and all their relatives under the one extended family umbrella. Gatherings of the *mespucha*, whether for birthdays, anniversaries, Bar Mitzvahs, weddings or funerals, were exciting, noisy and wonderful events with simultaneous conversations in Yiddish, Dutch and English with a host of European accents.

My mother's family was never orthodox and worshipped at the Reform Synagogue in the Oxford and St George's Club run by Sir Basil and Lady Henriques. This was a centre for religious, social and sporting activities for the whole of the poor Jewish community in the East End and our family was heavily involved in many aspects of this wonderful institution. Early in the war my parents and I moved out of London to the rural tranquillity of Tring in Hertfordshire. We didn't keep separate pans, dishes, cutlery and crockery for milk and meat, but my mother never served milk and meat together and no forbidden food ever entered her kitchen. Kosher meat and poultry came from London by train, or was brought by my father when he came back from work on Fridays, together with a selection of cousins who wanted a weekend in the country.

Opposite: *Kate and Louis van Straten, photographed by Baron, 13 September 1937.*
My mother made her wedding dress and the collar, sleeves and hem were beaded with rows of tiny seed pearls – every one sewn on by hand.
Below: *Me aged five with my mother and father. My mouth is firmly shut to hide missing front teeth, lost when I fell out of a taxi outside John Barnes in Finchley Road, now Waitrose.*

There was a number of Jewish families in Tring during the war, enough to run a small synagogue in a wonderful building that used to be the Gaiety Theatre and there was nearly always the required ten men (a *minyon*) to hold a formal service. After the war most returned to London, but my parents stayed for another 20 years. I was lucky enough to be educated at one of the oldest public schools in England in the nearby town of Berkhamsted. Unlike the author Graham Greene, who hated the school and whose father had been headmaster, I loved it and spent an extremely happy ten years there. In a total of 600 or more boys only six of us were Jews – they still had quotas in those days – but in spite of a bit of juvenile anti-Semitism, especially from the Irish Catholic lads, there was no discrimination within the school. A Rabbi came every Sunday morning to hold religious classes, which included two or three girls from our sister school, and that was our only alternative to attending the school chapel service.

Although no Kosher food was available, my wonderful housemaster, the late Monty Fry, understood the problems and whenever ham, pork, bacon or other forbidden foods were on the menu, there was always an alternative for me and the two other Jewish boys in the boarding house. The real fun started when I took hordes of my contemporaries home to mother. These were youngsters of every race, creed and colour whose far-flung homes in India, Africa, Asia and South America made family visits impossible for them. My mother adopted them all and whether I turned up with one or four extra mouths, she fed them. I meet old school friends today who, 50 years on, talk about my mother's wonderful cooking and how much at home they felt in the very Jewish atmosphere of our house.

As the only Jewish boy growing up in a very conservative small country town, life wasn't always easy and it was sometimes embarrassing to ask a friend's mother what was in the sandwiches, or what meat was in the stew, but they were all very understanding and soon learned that there were foods that I didn't eat. One terrible exception was being invited to join a girlfriend with her family at a very posh lunch in an expensive local restaurant. Her father was a large choleric man whose equally large moustache testified to his RAF service in the war, and was given to drinking Black Velvet – half Guinness, half champagne – out of a 1-pint silver mug early in the morning. I coped with the hors d'oeuvre as I managed to hide the prawns under the shredded lettuce and squash it all down so it looked as if I'd eaten them, but to my horror the main course was specially ordered Lobster Thermidore, which I had to turn down. The father ranted and raved and shouted so much that I left the room scarlet with embarrassment and didn't see his beautiful daughter, whom I thought was the love of my life, for another 40 years.

I can't claim to have led a blameless life of Kosher eating, but to this day I've never eaten shellfish or pork and can't imagine ever doing so.

Thanks to General Franco   If it weren't for the fascist dictator General Franco, I wouldn't be here. In the late 1930s my mother, her partner in their wedding-dress business and their best friend planned a holiday in Spain.

With bags packed and tickets booked, the best friend was refused a visa at the very last moment as she was born in Russia and had a Russian passport. The three smart young girls decided to go to Holland and in the seaside town of Scheveningen my mother met my father on the beach where he was a performing gymnast. In spite of not speaking a word of each other's language, they fell in love, my father followed her back to England and it wasn't long before they were married. I arrived in 1939.

I never knew my father's parents nor any of his enormous family, except for his youngest brother Jo. Though I owed my existence to one fascist, another took the lives of 150 members of my father's family – parents, grandparents, brothers, sisters, nieces, nephews, uncles, aunts and every other relative. My uncle Jo and his wife Henny were hidden by the most extraordinarily brave Catholic family in the cellars of their house, where they lived on potato peel, tulip bulbs and dead rats for two years.

I think for all Jews the taste, smell and sight of traditional foods are a window onto the very soul of Jewishness. Happily my mother spent enough time with her mother-in-law before the war to learn many of the skills of Dutch Jewish cooking, with its Asian and Iberian influences. For my father these 'tastes of home' were the links with his childhood and lost family. Food memories play a powerful role in the Jewish psyche, serving as reminders of past times, good and bad, of communities destroyed and families lost. When I cook one of my aunt Henny's recipes, the smells transport me to her tiny kitchen in Rotterdam; I can see the view across the lake from her window; I imagine sitting with my uncle Jo as a seven-year-old while he taught me to play chess; I relive the moment of stepping out of Rotterdam station in 1947 and seeing hardly a single building standing; I still feel the thrill of ice skating with the next-door neighbour's son along the canals to his school.

Thanks, I'm sure, to my mother's wonderful cooking and the huge love of her entire family, my father was an amazingly fit, strong and healthy man till he died at the age of 87. He never spoke to me about the loss of his family or the guilt he must have felt at having escaped the horrors of the Holocaust. To my great joy my father formed a very close bond with my second wife, Sally, a rather lapsed Irish Catholic. One evening they had a meal together and for no obvious reason he started to talk about his family, the war and his terrible sense of loss. Once he started there was no stopping and Sally said she hardly spoke a word for four hours. Father had received some letters written on the transport trains and from the death camps. He also spoke to some survivors about those terrible times, but I don't think he ever really came to terms with losing his family and every one of his contemporary school friends. Apart from his one surviving brother there was no one to whom he could say about his early years, 'Do you remember when...'

To this day Sally finds it hard to understand how Louis, my dad, could ever laugh or smile again after all that tragedy.

Above: *Dutch treat – my lovely mother, Kate (left) with her business partner, Elsie, and best friend Leah (right). This was taken on a girls' holiday in Holland in the summer of 1936. Just a few days later Kate met my father, they fell desperately in love and he followed her back to England.*

Going back to its roots

To Jews and non-Jews alike, the idea of a healthy Jewish cookbook must seem like the impossible dream. But how wrong can they be? The belief that all Jewish food is 'a heart attack on a plate' stems from limited encounters with the Jewish food of northern and eastern Europe. Heavy, fatty, salty or over-sweet dishes filled with chicken fat, salt beef, cream cheese, pickled herrings and strudel were the products only of 20th-century Europe.

The health hazards came with affluence. Having fuel and living in northern Europe, the UK and America reduced the enormous need for calories that were essential to survive the bitter winters of eastern Europe. Having money meant adding more meat and fewer vegetables, beans and grains to the stew or casserole. Gradually the physical demands of work declined so that today there is no longer a calorie requirement listed for 'heavy manual labour'. Machines have taken over and they need the calories, not the operators.

In earlier times food was scarce and rationed by lack of money and availability. Just like the British during the Second World War, food rationing meant a healthier diet. Even the dreaded *cholent*, with its artery-clogging saturated fat and heart-stoppingly massive portions served by mothers-in-law, started life as the healthiest of dishes. It originated in medieval France and, according to the great and academic food writer Claudia Roden, the name is derived from the French *chaud* and *lent,* which mean hot and slow respectively. It was taken to the village bakery on Friday afternoon and left to cook overnight, ready to collect at the end of the Sabbath day. This was a dish of beans, lentils and root vegetables and in the good times may have had a scrap of meat for flavour. But it was virtually fat-free.

In spite of this, the all-too-common perception of Jewish cooking has spread through the highly influential German-Jewish community of the early 20th century and the enormous influx of Jewish refugees fleeing the pogroms of eastern Europe and Russia from the mid 19th century onwards. But this ignores the Sephardi Jews, whose cultural and culinary contributions to Jewish eating have historically been underrated. In truth these are the Jews often overlooked by their Ashkenazi brethren. The Sephardim were Jews who settled in the Spanish peninsula, the Ottoman Empire – mainly Greece and Turkey – the north African countries of Morocco, Tunisia, Libya and Algeria, and finally there were those who went to Persia and Babylon. Fed by the Diaspora, these communities flourished and, whilst keeping to the Jewish dietary laws, they adopted the local foods and culinary traditions. The desert and its meagre produce defined the food of the Yemenite Jews, whereas in Mesopotamia, the heart of the fertile crescent which saw man's first successful agriculture, there were lush pastures, rich crops and abundant fish. Sephardi settlers around the Mediterranean adapted their cuisine to the Mediterranean climate and have produced some of the healthiest Jewish food of all. Jews travelled the

Baker's treat: Bagels and all sorts of other Jewish specialities were the foundation of Henry Goldring's shop in Upper Clapton Road, north London when it opened just around the turn of the 20th century.

silk routes and settled in China, communities grew up in India, in Persia, Egypt, east Africa and the Far East. Jewish cuisine spread and prospered but remained virtually unknown to the world of Ashkenazi Jewry.

The Ashkenazi Jews were those who moved further to the north and east, choosing to live in Germany, France, Italy and the United Kingdom. As the ravages of the Crusades forced them eastwards to escape slaughter and persecution, they ended up in Poland and Russia where, because of the extremely harsh climate, their food was very different. Not for them delicate spices, fruits and salads, but rib-sticking dishes of sauerkraut, root vegetables, dumplings, smoked and salted meat and fish.

Bagels, smoked salmon and cream cheese – real fusion food

As much as the innovative Australian chefs like to take the credit for the cooking cult of fusion food, I'm afraid they're wrong. Imaginative, inventive and wonderful though it is, their melding together of flavours from the Pacific Rim, Europe and Australia was pre-dated by several thousand years when the Red Sea parted and the Diaspora of Jews began. The strict requirements of Jewish dietary laws determined how Jews ate wherever they settled in the world and this resulted in the fusion of foods from many lands.

When the Jews travelled they took many of their creative culinary practices with them, so the hot spicy dishes from the Kosher kitchens of Cochin migrated to east Africa, whereas most South African Jews came from northern Europe, especially from Holland. This is where the fascinating pieces of the jigsaw start fitting together. Consider that the Cochin Jews were heavily involved in the spice trade, dealing especially in turmeric, cloves, nutmeg, cinnamon and pepper, and during the late 17th and most of the 18th centuries they worked with the highly successful Dutch East India Company. These exotic cargoes were stored in magnificent buildings lining the great canals of Amsterdam, then the centre of the European spice trade. Some of the Indian Jews ended up in Holland, but many other Dutch Jews came from Spain and Portugal, where the powerful effect of the Moorish occupation influenced the herbs and spices used in cooking. Still more Jews came to Holland from eastern Europe, bringing with them their tastes for sausage, sauerkraut and hearty winter dishes essential in such a bitter climate. They were using garlic, onion, caraway, dill, fennel, parsley and all the other north European culinary herbs.

Put all this into the same stockpot and you have the ultimate fusion cooking which became so popular that many dishes found their way into non-Jewish Dutch kitchens. When the Boers – Dutch farmers who were mostly non-conformist Christians – went to South Africa, together with both Ashkenazi and Sephardi Jews, they took with them a Europeanised form of Dutch-Indian-Moorish cooking which is commonplace throughout South Africa.

Purely by coincidence, I spent a number of years working in a therapy centre that occupied a wonderful 17th-century spice warehouse in Amsterdam. Though the building had not been used for its original purpose for more than 100 years, the magical aroma of spices had seeped into its very fabric. Often I was the only person there overnight, and in the small, still hours, when the building creaked and groaned on its 300-year-old wooden piles deep beneath the water, I could still smell the spices and imagine enormous heaps of hessian sacks bulging with their exotic cargo.

The popular image of the 'wandering Jew' is not far from the truth as it seems that almost every Jew has inherited the travelling gene and they move with equal ease from village to village or from town to town as they do from country to country or continent to continent. Whether forced by persecution and pogroms, or undertaken for purposes of trade and business or simply to satisfy a wanderlust, Jews have travelled to the four corners of the earth in the past 3,000 years. Wherever they end up, they take with them the religious demands of the Kosher kitchen and the culinary traditions of the place they leave and merge these two, seamlessly, with the food available in their new homes.

Nowhere is this more obvious than in New York, the original mecca of American Jewry. In the early 1900s European Jews flooded into America, mostly arriving in New York with little more than the clothes they stood in. It was here that Ashkenazi Jewish cooking had the most profound effect on the eating habits of the American nation. Husbands, brothers, cousins, fathers and even grandfathers were the first to arrive and it was their task to find work and homes so their families could follow. To serve the huge appetites of these hardworking single men, the New York deli was born. These Jewish-run Kosher eateries gave these men their tastes of home: barley soup you could stand a spoon in; salt beef and pastrami in doorstep sandwiches; stuffed cabbage; sauerkraut; *gefilte* fish – boiled or fried fishcakes; salamis and sausages of every shape; chopped liver; pickled herrings and smoked salmon, all served with mountains of rye bread and dill pickles. As the Jews spread across America they took their delis with them and they soon became the place to eat for every immigrant group that followed.

These are the roots of fusion cooking.

Healthy Kosher food

I've tried to find the healthiest of Kosher Jewish recipes to include in this book, but I've also endeavoured to make sure that they're simple and delicious. This I hope will encourage Jews to eat more healthily and non-Jews to enjoy these fascinating foods, some of which date back to almost a thousand years before the Christian era, and which combine the traditions of Jewish cooking with flavours from the entire world. That said, the basic principles of Kosher cooking are healthy, particularly those which forbid the consumption of milk and meat foods in the same meal. This simple practice immediately reduces the amount of saturated and artery-clogging fat consumed. If you want to finish your dinner with cheese, you must eat low-fat fish rather than meat. If you want cream on your fruit salad, tart or pudding, then you may not eat sausage, hamburger, salami or any other form of meat beforehand.

From the biblical lands flowing with milk and honey, Jewish cooks have had a love affair with good food. Every fruit and vegetable, nuts, seeds and all manner of grains, herbs and spices feature in the repertoire of Jewish cooking. Sea and fresh-water fish, olive oil, scrupulous attention to hygiene, the religious requirements of the dietary laws and the mandatory, frequent washing of hands all contribute to the healthiness of the best of Jewish cooking.

Dried fruits have always been a favourite and these are highly concentrated sources of powerfully protective nutrients. The foods which are your best defence against heart disease, high blood pressure, strokes, many forms of cancer, arthritis and ageing are those with the highest ORAC scores. ORAC (Oxygen Radical Absorbance Capacity) is a way of measuring the protective value of whole foods devised by scientists at Tufts University Research Centre on Ageing in Boston, USA. Best are the dark-coloured fruits and vegetables. The average British diet provides about 1,500 ORAC units a day, but optimum protection comes from 5,000 units. Blueberries, strawberries, spinach, Brussels sprouts, plums, dried apricots, raisins and garlic are abundant in these plant chemicals, but richest of all are prunes. Throughout the book you'll find useful information in the introductions to the recipes.

For the ultra-orthodox Jew there is no compromise over the laws of Kashrut and anyone that observant will not need detailed explanations of the dietary laws. But just to paint a broad picture of what is involved in Kosher eating, here are some of the basic facts. The basic laws of Kashrut were handed down by God to the Jews, sanctified in the holy scroll of the Torah and amplified by generations of Rabbis throughout the centuries. These laws are accepted without question and although it's possible to find reasons of health and hygiene within the biblical commandments, Rabbis tell us that it's pointless to search for deeper meanings. The laws of Kashrut are God's words and need no questioning.

Fishy story: In London's East End, fish was a staple diet food for much of the Jewish population. Obviously not Kosher – orthodox Jews don't eat oysters – Henry Phillips, seen here with three of his children, was a popular member of the local community. This picture was taken in 1950.

Meat   The only meat allowed comes from animals with cloven feet that chew the cud. So ox, cow, veal, mutton, lamb, goat and the more exotic gazelle, antelope and mountain sheep are all allowed, as theoretically is venison. These animals must be slaughtered in the ritual manner by having their throats cut and this must be done under the supervision of an approved *shochet* (slaughterer). It's widely believed that the hindquarters cannot be eaten, which is why it's seldom possible to eat a good Kosher steak. This is not true as, if properly prepared by having the sciatic nerve removed, they would be permissible.

Deli desire: Salt beef, gefilte fish, chopped liver, egg and onions and a variety of sandwiches were on sale at Abrahamson's restaurant in London's theatreland. This photograph was taken in the early 1930s.

In the Jewish religion the most potent symbol of life is blood and its consumption is absolutely forbidden, which is why all blood must be drained immediately at the time of slaughter. The meat then has to be soaked and salted or, in the case of offal like liver, grilled under a very high heat so that no blood remains.

Poultry   Chicken, duck, turkey and goose are permitted, but all birds of prey and scavengers are not. Game birds that have been hunted or wild fowl are not Kosher unless they've been bred and slaughtered in the ritual manner.

Fish   Kosher fish must have removable scales and fins, so all shellfish and crustaceans, along with octopus, squid, eels, monkfish, ray, rock salmon, skate, sturgeon, swordfish and turbot are amongst those not regarded as being Kosher.

Dairy products   These may not be consumed at the same time as meat, though the length of time you should wait does vary from one community to another. You can't cook meat and milk together, and the period after meat before you can consume milk ranges from two to six hours. You can eat a dairy meal and then a meat meal without a waiting period, but a milk-based starter and a meat main course would not be acceptable. There are non-dairy substitutes like Kosher margarine, non-dairy creamers and milk substitutes, but they are generally high in saturated fats, extremely unhealthy and I don't ever use them. Soya products are a great alternative and certified Kosher versions are more widely available now. For the strictly orthodox, it's necessary to use Kosher cheese, which is made without animal rennet, and it's also important to avoid dairy products like yogurts which contain animal-based gelatine.

Pareve foods   These are foods that are neither meat nor dairy and can be eaten with any type of meal. They include all fruits and vegetables, grains, eggs and fish (see above), but of course if you cook them with butter or animal fat, or serve them with a cream sauce, they then become milk or meat foods.

The religious festivals

There are many Jewish festivals that have their own food rituals. To the orthodox Jew they all have immense importance, but to all Jews, even the least observant, there are some that never lose their significance. The enduring qualities of *Shabbat* – the ushering-in of Sabbath on Friday night – are the cornerstone of Judaism, bringing light, blessings and peace. As one of the ten commandments, observing the Sabbath is the Jew's acknowledgement that God created the world in six days and rested on the seventh. Lighting the candles, blessing the bread and wine and sitting down with the family on Friday night is an instantly recognisable ceremony wherever Jews are found, even in the farthest outposts of human occupation.

No matter how simple, humble, rich or poor the table may be, it is the custom to cover it with a white cloth. Add the Sabbath candlesticks and the altar-like symbolism is immediately apparent. These rituals all help to reinforce the religious aspects of these ceremonial meals. The mother's traditional blessing of the Sabbath candles and the presence of the entire family around the 'altar' are the catalyst which hardens the cement binding families and communities together. The universality of the language of Jewish prayer makes a stranger feel at home at a Sabbath table or a synagogue anywhere in the world. I've always felt that the Catholic church made a great mistake when they abandoned the Latin mass which made it accessible to worshippers in every country.

There are many festivals throughout the year. Here are details of just a few of the most important. New Year and Yom Kippur (the Day of Atonement) have deep meanings for even the least-observant Jews. Those who hardly ever set foot inside a synagogue will do so on one of those days.

Rosh Hashanah – New Year   This occurs on the first and second days of the Hebrew month *Tishrei*, which is normally in September or October. At this time, Jews throughout the world pray for a new year of health, peace and prosperity. It's a time of judgement and a time when we seek God's guidance to help us live better lives in the year to come.

This is also the time when the *Shofar* (ram's horn) is blown in the synagogue – a hundred blasts during the two days of services. This is the most ancient of all wind instruments and its plaintive sound is highly symbolic. During this festival it's traditional to eat sweet foods as an indication of sweet things to come in the New Year. *Challah* (plaited loaf covered in poppy seeds) is dipped in honey, slices of apple coated with honey, sweet fresh fruits and *tzimmes* (carrots cooked with honey and orange juice) are all eaten. The meal is often finished with a pomegranate in the hope that our good deeds may increase like the seeds of this delicious fruit. Honey cake is another traditional New Year treat.

Yom Kippur   This is the most solemn day in the Jewish calendar, ten days after New Year. It begins just before sunset and until sunset the next day it's forbidden to eat or drink. The orthodox also abstain from sex, using perfumes and wearing leather shoes. This is a time of confession, memorial prayers for the dead and judgement for the coming year. At the end of the fast the whole family gathers for a meal of true celebration.

Sukkot   Taking place on the 15th and 16th of the Hebrew month Tishrei, this is the Jewish equivalent of harvest festival. Traditionally, Jews build a covered shelter outside where for a week all meals are eaten. The roof should be made of evergreen branches like laurel, ivy, leylandii or any other suitable plant material and the walls could be plywood, plastic sheeting, canvas or any other temporary material, though some part of the roof must be open to the sky. The building of this *sukkah* is very much a part of the festival.

Chanukah   This begins on the 25th day of the Hebrew month *Kislev*, corresponding to November/December, and frequently coincides with Christmas.

The great symbol of Chanukah is the *menorah*, a candlestick with eight branches and a separate holder for the candle used to light the others. Here we celebrate the victory of a tiny band of Maccabees against the entire Greek army. After defeating the Greeks they set about restoring the defiled holy temple but they could find only one tiny jar of oil that hadn't been defiled by the invading soldiers and it was enough to light the *menorah* for just one day. But a miracle occurred and the oil burned for eight whole days, after which freshly pressed oil was prepared. This miracle celebrates the defeat of the Greeks who were desperate to discredit the Jewish deity and convert all to the worship of their gods. Each night a candle is lit and by the eighth night all eight illuminate the home.

Because of the oil, this is when fried foods are popular - potato *latkes* (pancakes), small fried doughnuts and cheese *latkes* are common foods. This is also a time when children get presents including money, some of which they are expected to give to charity.

Pesach   Passover is celebrated from the 15th to the 22nd of the Hebrew month *Nissan*, corresponding to March/April, and often coincides with Easter. This is the great celebration of the exodus from ancient Egypt and the giving of the law on Mount Sinai. As the Jews left Egypt the Egyptians were afflicted by the plagues, the sea opened to let the Jews pass, then closed over the pursuing Egyptian horsemen. Passover celebrates this deliverance from bondage and the most important religious service takes place in the home. This is the time when no leavened bread but only *matzo* is eaten. These flat crisp sheets of baked dough are a reminder that when the Jews fled Egypt there was no time to let the bread rise, so it was made without yeast and baked like biscuits. The *Seder* service, as it is known, takes place with family, friends and neighbours seated round the dining table on the first two evenings of Passover. The story of the exodus is retold, mainly for benefit of the children so that each generation can pass it on to the next.

Six special foods are eaten, normally arranged on a plate designed to hold them. These are roasted chicken neck or lamb shank representing the Paschal lamb eaten on the eve of the exodus; a hard-boiled egg for the offering in the holy temple; bitter herbs (usually fresh horseradish, chicory or bitter green leaves), lest we forget the bitterness and slavery of our ancestors in Egypt; *charoset*, chopped apples, nuts and red wine mixed to remind us how the Jews laboured under Pharaoh to make bricks without straw; a non-bitter vegetable like raw onion or potato; and finally, extra bitter herbs are made into a sandwich with *matzo*.

Although not a religious requirement, it's common for hard-boiled eggs to be served in salt water as a reminder of the tears shed for the suffering of the Jews in bondage and of the Egyptians who perished in the plagues and the sea.

The meal itself is eaten interspersed with various readings and songs from the Passover book, the *Haggadah*.

This service is of great importance in the religious upbringing of all Jewish children, but as families become more dispersed and communities less cohesive, there are now many communal *Seder* services conducted under the auspices of synagogues and a variety of Jewish organisations. Any Jew who hasn't sat through a *Seder* for years, or any non-Jew who has never been to one but has a Jewish friend, should try to participate in this, one of the most uplifting and meaningful of religious celebrations.

Salt and pepper pots These earthenware containers were made in Leeds around 1820. Meals are a very important part of Judaism and are treated almost as a religious occasion. The table symbolises the altar at the temple for the show bread. The inscription on the pot on the far left says, 'This is the table which is before the Lord' while the inscription on the other pot is from Numbers and Deuteronomy and is a quote from the *Shema*, the most important of the Jewish prayers, 'And you shall eat and you shall bless the Lord your God.'

starters

Radishes and quail's eggs

Serves 4

24 quail's eggs

24 smallish radishes, trimmed

75g (3oz) unsalted butter,
softened

1 level teaspoon celery salt
or 2 tablespoons celery seeds,
crushed

Although quail are biblical birds, they were almost certainly never bred in the Middle East, but were trapped in their exhausted state after migrating across the Mediterranean. These small birds, related to the pheasant, were native to parts of Europe and China. Their culinary history goes back to ancient Rome. Quail were, and still are, popular in France for their eggs as well as their meat.

In this recipe, the eggs are combined with radishes in the traditional French way of eating radishes with butter and salt.

Method Put the eggs into cold water, bring quickly to the boil and simmer for 4 minutes. Plunge immediately into cold water and leave to cool for about 3 minutes. Peel carefully.

Arrange the eggs and radishes alternately on a serving dish. If using butter and celery salt, mix the salt into the butter.

Serve the eggs and radishes in the middle of the table with the celery butter in a separate dish. If using butter and celery seeds, serve in separate bowls for dipping.

Health note Radishes stimulate liver function, and each quail egg provides 158 calories, protein and lots of iron and vitamin A as well as B vitamins.

Egg and onion with coriander

Serves 3–4

4 hard-boiled eggs, well mashed

6 medium spring onions, trimmed
and finely chopped

2 tablespoons extra-virgin olive oil

Black pepper

1 tablespoon finely chopped
coriander leaves

Here's another very traditional Jewish appetiser that is equally at home at a Bar Mitzvah, wedding or funeral. I'm sure previous generations weren't aware of the benefits of combining egg with onion, but in fact all members of the allium genus (onions, garlic, shallots, spring onions, leeks and chives) contain natural chemicals that help the body's elimination of cholesterol.

This dish is normally made with parsley, but an Indian Jewish friend always uses coriander in her recipe and it gives an unexpected peppery bite.

Method Mix together the eggs and onions. Drizzle on the olive oil and mix well. Season with pepper to taste. Serve sprinkled with the chopped coriander.

Chickpeas on spinach

Serves 2-3

1kg (2¼lb) baby spinach
25g (1oz) unsalted butter
200g (7oz) canned chickpeas
*   (drained weight)*
1 large sprig of sage
4 tablespoons extra-virgin olive oil
Black pepper

Throughout the Middle East, chickpeas are a staple food, as they are in India, Latin America, Spain and Italy. Like all the legumes, they're inexpensive, highly nutritious and amazing value for money. They're low in calories, virtually fat-free and an excellent source of fibre, especially the soluble fibre which is so important in controlling cholesterol levels.

Method Wash the spinach (even if it's 'ready-washed'). Melt the butter in a large pan. Add the spinach with just the water clinging to its leaves. Cover and heat gently, shaking the pan occasionally, until the spinach wilts – about 5 minutes.

Meanwhile, drain the chickpeas and rinse thoroughly. Put into a separate pan with the sage, add just enough water to cover and heat through gently for about 5-6 minutes.

Drain the spinach well, arrange on serving plates and drizzle over half the olive oil.

Drain the chickpeas, removing the sage, and divide between the serving plates on the spinach.

Drizzle over the remainder of the oil and season with black pepper to taste.

Health note Chickpeas contain lots of folic acid, protein and complex carbohydrates, so have a low glycaemic index, which means they provide slow-release energy and cause a minimal increase in blood-sugar levels and insulin production. For this reason, they help protect against type-2 diabetes. Chickpeas also contain a group of chemicals called isoflavones: oestrogen-like compounds that reduce the risk of osteoporosis and other symptoms of the menopause.

Avocado-stuffed tomatoes

Serves 4

4 beef tomatoes (or 8 smaller
* ones)*
2 medium avocados
4 spring onions, finely sliced
1 small garlic clove, finely chopped
Juice of 1 small lemon
Pinch of paprika
2 dashes of Tabasco sauce

For modern Jews, the popularity of the avocado is the result of the massive cultivation of this amazing fruit in Israel and California. It's most unfortunate that so many people think of the avocado as a high-fat, high-calorie and unhealthy food, when the exact opposite is true. This luscious, creamy fruit is probably the healthiest of all; ounce for ounce, it's the most nutritious of all the most popular fruits. There's also hardly any sodium in this recipe and it's wonderful food for children of all ages.

Method Slice the tops off the tomatoes, scoop out the insides and discard the tough membranes but reserve the pulp. Dry the cases gently with kitchen paper.

Halve the avocados and scrape the flesh into a bowl. Add the tomato pulp and the remainder of the ingredients and mash well.

Spoon into the tomato cases.

Health note Avocados provide 60 per cent more potassium than bananas, lots of magnesium (for energy), folic acid, fibre, riboflavin and vitamins B6, C and E. Most of the fat is monounsaturated, which lowers the dangerous LDL cholesterol and raises the heart-protective HDL cholesterol. Avocado is also one of the richest sources of beta-sitosterol, which helps lower blood pressure.

Peanuts with green beans

Serves 4

3 tablespoons olive oil

1 onion, finely chopped

*1 large garlic clove, very finely
    chopped*

*110g (4oz) unsalted, shelled
    peanuts*

*500g (18oz) string beans, trimmed
    and cut into 2.5cm (1in) lengths*

1 small green pepper, diced

Salt and black pepper

*1 tablespoon each finely chopped
    flat-leaf parsley and coriander*

This is a typical recipe from the remarkable black Jews of Ethiopia. They lived in virtual isolation until the Israelis brought them back to Israel in an amazing rescue operation which began with 12,000 in 1984 and culminated in 1991, when the remaining 14,000 were repatriated by the Israeli government. Known as Falashas – now considered a derogatory term by Ethiopian Jews – they believe they're descendants of Menelik, the son of King Solomon and the Queen of Sheba. This recipe is an example of reverse migration, as the Ethiopians brought their ancient traditions back to the land of their forefathers.

Method Heat the oil in a heavy frying pan and sauté the onion, garlic and nuts gently until the onions are soft. Add the beans and green pepper and continue to cook, stirring continuously, until the beans are tender, adding a little more olive oil if necessary. Season to taste.

Serve with the herbs scattered on top.

Health note Contrary to popular perception, peanuts are extremely healthy, as they provide slow-release energy, protect against diabetes and help with any weight-loss regime.

Brazilian bean salad

Serves 4-6

400g (14oz) quinoa, well rinsed
 and drained
500g (18oz) French green beans,
 topped and tailed
Salt
1 tablespoon pumpkin seeds
1 tablespoon sesame seeds
3 tablespoons extra-virgin olive oil
Juice of 1 lemon

Before travelling up the Amazon to study the medicinal herbs of the rain forest Indians, I spent a few days in Rio where I went to a jewellery shop to buy my wife a present. The owner turned out to be Jewish and invited me to join his family for the Sabbath meal on Friday evening. That was my first introduction to quinoa. Like buckwheat, this isn't a grain but the seed from a very distant relative of spinach. Cultivated for more than 5,000 years in South America, it was the staple food of the Incas. Although it's a fairly recent arrival in Europe and America, you'll find it ready-prepared in health stores and good supermarkets.

Method Toast the quinoa in a dry frying pan, stirring continuously for 3-4 minutes. Put it into a large saucepan, cover with 700ml (1^{1}/4 pints) cold water, bring to the boil, cover and simmer until translucent, when the germ spirals out of each grain (about 15 minutes), adding extra boiling water if necessary. Drain if necessary and leave to cool.

Boil the beans in lightly salted water until *al dente* – about 2 minutes. Refresh in cold water and drain. Mix together the quinoa and beans and sprinkle with the pumpkin and sesame seeds. Drizzle with the olive oil. Pour on the lemon juice to taste.

Health note Quinoa is extremely rich in iron and potassium, and also contains B vitamins, zinc and magnesium. Unlike most grains, it provides almost complete protein (as well as being delicious to eat).

Falafel

Serves 4

110g (4oz) dried chickpeas
110g (4oz) canned chickpeas
   (drained weight)
1 teaspoon paprika
1 teaspoon celery seeds, crushed
1 tablespoon finely chopped fresh
   coriander leaves
1 tablespoon finely chopped
   flat-leaf parsley
1 garlic clove, crushed
1 medium onion, chopped
About 125ml (4fl oz) rapeseed or
   olive oil
1 Iceberg lettuce, finely shredded
   or Cos lettuce leaves
4 plum tomatoes, chopped
Lemon slices, to garnish

This ancient dish has its origins shrouded in antiquity. In many parts of the Middle East, it was traditionally made from dried broad beans (fava), which are a staple of Lebanese cuisine. It was probably the Yemenite Jews who first introduced falafel to Israel, although it was, in fact, one of the most popular foods of the Palestinians. So quickly did these delicious nuggets of chickpeas, herbs and spices endear themselves to the Israelis that as early as the celebrations of their first independence day, 14 May 1947, there were falafel sellers in Zion Square providing food for the gathered crowds.

For the orthodox Jew, falafel is one of the useful *pareve* foods – meaning they can be eaten with either milk or meat meals. This home-made delicacy is entirely different from those heavy, dense and often greasy commercial products. It is definitely worth the time and effort.

Method Soak the chickpeas in water for at least 8 hours. Drain and whizz them in a food-processor with the canned chickpeas, spices, herbs, garlic and onion. Don't overprocess, otherwise you'll end up with a purée that makes a very dense falafel. Taking a tablespoon at a time, make the mixture into balls about the size of a walnut.

Heat the oil in a wok or deep frying pan and fry the falafels in batches until golden – about 5 minutes per batch. Drain each batch on kitchen paper and keep warm until all the mixture is used.

Serve on a bed of shredded lettuce, topped with chopped tomatoes and garnished with lemon slices.

Spiced aubergine purée

This wonderful purée is a typical food of the Jewish people who came from Iraq during the 17th century. They settled in Calcutta, where they prospered and, typical of Jews all over the world, soon fused their culinary skills with the traditions of their adopted homeland. Sadly, their community is now quite small, but the traditional bread made by Jewish bakers is still produced today in non-Jewish bakeries – but not on Saturdays. You can follow their traditions and eat this purée with Indian breads such as naan and chapatti.

Method Put the aubergines in a colander, sprinkling the layers with salt to encourage the expulsion of excess water. Leave for an hour, then rinse thoroughly and wipe dry with kitchen paper.

Put the ginger and chilli into a small food-processor and blitz until smooth.

Heat the oil in a large pan and gently sauté the onion and garlic until soft. Stir in the ginger/chilli paste and continue cooking for 2 minutes. Add the turmeric, coriander, cumin and half the garam masala and cook for another minute, stirring continuously. Add the tomatoes and continue cooking and stirring for 1 more minute.

Tip in the aubergines, turn down the heat and simmer, covered, until the dish resembles a purée – about 1 hour – adding a small amount of water if it seems as if it's drying out. Add the remainder of the garam masala, stirring it in well for about 5 minutes. Check the seasoning and serve with naan and/or chapatti.

Tabbouleh

Serves 4-6

225g (8oz) bulgur wheat, rinsed,
soaked in cold water for
30 minutes and thoroughly
drained
1 large red onion, finely chopped
3 heaped tablespoons crushed
walnuts
8 cherry tomatoes, halved
1 cucumber, peeled, deseeded and
diced
2 tablespoons finely chopped
flat-leaf parsley leaves
1 tablespoon finely chopped
coriander leaves
2 tablespoons finely chopped
mint leaves
Juice of 2 lemons
4 tablespoons extra-virgin olive oil
1 Cos lettuce
12 olives, a mixture of black and
green, pitted and halved
Wholemeal pitta bread, to serve

There are as many recipes for tabbouleh among the Jews of the Middle East and north Africa as there are for colcannon among the Catholics of southern Ireland. Israeli Jews have adopted a style that has much more bulgur wheat than other ingredients, whereas in other parts of the Middle East, especially Lebanon, it looks more like a green salad. This recipe is somewhere in the middle, with the added slightly bitter bite of walnuts.

Method Tip the bulgur wheat into a large bowl. Using a large spoon, mix in the onion and walnuts. Add the tomatoes, cucumber, parsley, coriander and mint and stir again. Pour on the lemon juice and olive oil and mix in well.

Arrange the lettuce leaves like the spokes of a wheel on a large platter and tip in the tabbouleh. Scatter the olives on top.

Serve with the pitta bread.

Health note: Bulgur wheat is a highly nutritious wholegrain cereal providing protein, fibre and B vitamins. Made like this, tabbouleh overflows with heart-protective and cancer-preventative phytonutrients as well as the digestive benefits of mint and coriander.

Chopped herring with apple

Serves 4

2 salted herring fillets
2 pickled herring fillets
2 hard-boiled eggs, finely chopped
1 medium white onion, very finely
  chopped
1 apple, peeled, cored and grated
2 tablespoons matzo meal
1 teaspoon brown caster sugar
2 tablespoons lemon juice
2 tablespoons cider vinegar
Ground white pepper

What could be more Jewish than chopped herring – one of the healthiest recipes brought from eastern Europe? This dish may seem like a lot of work, but I promise you it's worth it: totally different from any commercial product. And if you're not Jewish and have never tasted this icon of Kosher cooking, get chopping. And I mean chopping – not shoving it in a blender, where it loses its wonderful texture. This is a slightly healthier version of my Aunt Gertie's recipe, with much less sugar and no added salt, and is best eaten with traditional Jewish rye bread made with caraway seeds.

Method Put the fish on a large chopping board and chop until fine. Put into a serving bowl, add the eggs, onion and apple and mix well.

Sprinkle on the matzo meal and sugar and mix again. Add the lemon juice and vinegar and stir well. Season to taste with ground white pepper.

Health note Herring simply oozes good health, as it's full of essential fatty acids for brain function, protein and lots of vitamin D, which is essential for strong bones; your body needs it in order to absorb calcium.

Schmaltz herrings

Serves 4

4 schmaltz or matjes herring fillets,
   cut into 2.5cm (1in) slices
4 medium tomatoes, sliced
1 cucumber, peeled and sliced
1 small red onion, very finely
   sliced
Juice of 1 small lemon
1 tablespoon olive oil
Black pepper
1 tablespoon chopped parsley

For European and American Jews, herring is probably the most important fish. Its popularity, which began in eastern Europe and Germany, has been taken wherever these Jews migrated. For them, herring was never out of season, and when it was not available fresh, they devised many ways of preserving it so that this healthy fish could be eaten year-round.

When I was young, one of my many uncles owned a very famous Kosher deli in Petticoat Lane, the heart of London's East End Jewish community. Most Sunday mornings I went there with my father and to this day I can close my eyes and smell that wonderful shop: wooden barrels full of pickled cucumbers, sacks of bagels hot from the bakery around the corner. While my father shopped, my treat was a bagel with schmaltz herring.

The traditional schmaltz herring is made from mature fish (which has a higher fat content), filleted and preserved in brine. The Dutch matjes herring is a younger fish, skinned, filleted and preserved in a mix of brine, sugar and vinegar. Either way, this recipe makes a wonderfully delicious starter or light meal; as the latter, it was traditionally served with warm, boiled potatoes.

Method Arrange the fish, tomato and cucumber slices alternately in a dish. Scatter the sliced onion on top.

Mix together the lemon juice, olive oil and black pepper to taste and pour over the dish. Serve with the chopped parsley scattered on top.

Smoked white fish salad

Serves 4-6

900g (2lb) smoked whitefish
  (easily available in the US and in
  some fishmongers in the UK) or
  other smoked white fish, such as
  halibut or cod
4 tablespoons live natural yogurt
4 tablespoons mascarpone cheese
1 Ogen melon, peeled, deseeded
  and cut into cubes
2 celery sticks, finely chopped
1 small red onion, finely chopped
Juice of 1 lemon
1 Little Gem lettuce
4 tablespoons finely snipped chives

Smoking, salting and sun-drying were the earliest methods of preserving fish, although pickling, suitable for oily fish like herring, became popular in Europe towards the end of the 19th century. Smoked salmon, haddock and kippers were appreciated in the UK, but salmon became the hallmark of Jews in London's East End. Smoked whitefish was never as important as it became in Europe or in the delis of New York.

I was given this wonderful, nutritious salad, very low in saturated fats and rich in everything else, in the London home of a Danish Jewish family, where it was made with smoked halibut.

Method Break the fish into bite-sized pieces. Mix together the yogurt and mascarpone cheese and carefully fold in the fish.

Put the melon, celery and onion into a bowl. Add lemon juice to taste. Gently fold the fish into the salad. Arrange on individual plates on a bed of Little Gem leaves.

Serve sprinkled with the chives.

Tuna roll

Serves 4

400g (14oz) canned tuna in oil (undrained weight)

4 tablespoons grated Parmesan cheese

2 large eggs, well beaten

10 heaped tablespoons medium matzo meal

Mayonnaise, to serve

Until the Second World War, there was a large orthodox Jewish community in Rome. Its members combined typical Italian ingredients such as tuna and Parmesan cheese to make this version of the traditional boiled *gefilte* fish.

Gefilte is the Yiddish word for filled or stuffed, and is used to describe many different dishes. The original fish balls used to be poached and served stuffed into the skin of the fish.

Method Put the tuna, with its oil, into a large bowl with the Parmesan cheese, eggs and matzo meal. Mash well with a fork. Make into a sausage shape and wrap in muslin or clingfilm.

Poach in a large pan of simmering water for 30 minutes, until set. Remove from the pan and chill. Serve sliced, with mayonnaise – preferably home-made, or use your own favourite commercial variety.

Health note This is a high-protein recipe which also contains calcium, B vitamins and a relatively small proportion of carbohydrates.

Italian tuna toasts

Serves 6

About 185g (6¹/₂oz) canned tuna in
  olive oil (undrained weight)
3 canned anchovy fillets, finely
  chopped
50g (2oz) unsalted butter, at room
  temperature, cubed
1 teaspoon chopped fresh oregano
  (dried won't do)
Juice and zest of 1 lemon
Black pepper
1 standard ciabatta loaf, sliced
  lengthways and each half cut into
  three pieces
Peeled cucumber
Mixed black and green pitted olives

Olives and ciabatta make this unmistakably a dish of Italy, where it has long been a favourite of the Jewish community. This delicious starter will work with mackerel or any canned or chunky smoked fish. Serve with peeled cucumber with mixed black and green pitted olives

Method Put the tuna, with its oil, into a food-processor and whizz until it breaks up. Add the anchovies, butter, oregano and lemon zest and whizz until smooth. Season to taste with lemon juice and black pepper.

Toast the ciabatta pieces and pile the tuna mixture on top. Mix together the cucumber and olives and serve on the side.

Health note The essential fatty acids from the fish are not only good brain food, but may also help with problems such as attention deficit hyperactivity disorder (ADHD) and dyslexia. This dish is a good source of vitamin D, which is important for the prevention of osteoporosis as it improves the absorption of calcium.

Trout and mushroom piroshki

Serves 6-8

4 tablespoons olive oil

1 onion, finely chopped

110g (4oz) trout fillet, cut into thin batons along the grain of the fish

110g (4oz) wild mushrooms, heads only, wiped clean and finely chopped

125ml (4fl oz) vegetable stock – see recipe for Barley with mushrooms and marjoram (page 47) or use a good-quality, low-salt cube or bouillon powder such as Kallo or Marigold

1 sprig each of thyme, rosemary and parsley

350ml (12fl oz) crème fraîche

1 heaped tablespoon chopped dill

1 heaped tablespoon finely snipped chives

500g (18oz) frozen vegetarian shortcrust pastry, thoroughly thawed

Nothing could be more authentically Ashkenazi than this Russian *piroshki*. Unlike the New York Jewish street food, which was traditionally a bite-sized snack (known there as a *knish*), this is a large parcel wrapped in pastry and is equally delicious hot or cold.

Surprisingly, the first time I ate this dish I wasn't at home, but at one of many memorable meals I enjoyed with my father in one of his favourite restaurants. A Jewish white Russian émigré friend served it in its traditional Russian form as *koulibiac* every Friday night in his London restaurant. There, it was made with a whole salmon.

Method Preheat the oven to 200°C/400°F/gas mark 6. Heat 2 tablespoons of the oil in a large pan and gently sauté the onion until soft. Tip the onion and oil into a bowl. Put the remainder of the oil in the pan, add the trout and fry gently until it turns whitish – about 20 seconds. Add to the onion.

Tip the onion-and-trout juices back into the pan and add the mushrooms, stock and thyme, rosemary and parsley. Simmer for 3 minutes. Fish out the mushrooms and add to the onion and trout. Strain the stock, then reduce over a high heat until you have about 1 tablespoon left. Stir in the crème fraîche, onion, trout, mushrooms, dill and chives.

Roll out the pastry and cut into 10cm (4in) circles. Brush the edges with water. Put about a tablespoon of the mixture in the centre of each circle, fold the pastry over and seal the edges. Bake for 20 minutes.

Health note Scientists have now proved the truth of the old saying that fish is good for the brain. All oily fish provide essential fatty acids which improve brain function and protect the central nervous system.

Warm smoked salmon with raspberries

Serves 2-3

275g (10oz) smoked salmon, cut in
  1 thick slice
4 tablespoons balsamic vinegar
1 bunch watercress
1/2 fennel bulb, thinly sliced
  lengthways
1 small punnet raspberries (about
  20 fruits)
Black pepper
Wasabi (a hot green paste made
  from Japanese sea cabbage)
1 lemon, quartered

This recipe came from a Jewish friend who worked for some years in Japan. It's his adaptation of sushi, which, thanks to the oily fish, makes a healthy, high-protein starter that is so attractive to look at. Wasabi has a wonderful hot and sweet flavour and is also believed to have cancer-fighting properties. How different can you get from the traditional plate of smoked salmon?

Method Cut the smoked salmon into batons about 2.5cm (1in) long. Put into a small, wide pan with the balsamic vinegar and heat gently, stirring lightly, for 1 minute. Remove from the heat.

On individual plates, make mounds of the watercress, then the fennel, then the raspberries. Arrange the warm smoked salmon batons on top. Pour over the warm balsamic vinegar. Give each dish a twist of black pepper. Put a generous teaspoon of wasabi on the side of each plate.

Serve garnished with the lemon quarters.

Greek chicken patties

Serves 6

*4 skinned boneless chicken
breasts – or use meat left over
from making Chicken soup with
matzo dumplings (see page 66)*
1 medium onion, quartered
*3 teaspoons chopped dill or
fennel fronds*
3 tablespoons fine matzo meal
3 eggs, well beaten
About 100ml (3¹/2fl oz) olive oil
1 Iceberg lettuce, finely sliced

There have been Jews in Greece since ancient times. As happened wherever
Jews settled, they adapted local ingredients and cooking styles to the laws
of Kosher eating. These patties are equally delicious cold, make good party
canapés and they're an ideal healthy food to include in children's lunchboxes.

Method If using uncooked chicken breasts, cut them into slivers and poach
in a little seasoned water until tender – about 5 minutes. Grind the chicken
with the onion in a food-processor or put through a mincer. Put into a bowl
and mix well. Add the dill or fennel, matzo meal and eggs, and mix well again.

Wet your hands and, taking a large spoonful at a time, mould into small
patties.

Heat the olive oil until nearly smoking. Sauté the patties gently in the oil,
turning once, until golden. Cool slightly and serve on the lettuce.

Health note Full of protein,
B vitamins and minerals, these
patties are low in saturated fats.
The dill or fennel makes them
extremely easy to digest,

Chicken livers with grapes

Serves 2–3

2 tablespoons olive oil
2 shallots, very finely chopped
*350g (12oz) chicken livers (fresh
are best, but frozen will do),
all membranes removed*
About 3 tablespoons flour
1/2 glass red wine
*12 seedless grapes (red or white),
halved*
2–3 slices toast
*2 tablespoons finely chopped
parsley*

The traditional Jewish cook had the typical peasant approach to a chicken:
nothing was wasted. The feet, neck and giblets were all used in one way or
another, as was the liver. Rather than the ubiquitous chopped liver, however,
why not try this quick and healthy recipe popular with the Jewish community
in the south of France?

Method Heat the oil in a pan and sauté the shallots gently until soft. Cut the
chicken livers into bite-sized pieces, if necessary, and roll in the flour. Add to
the pan and cook, stirring continuously, until cooked right through – about
5 minutes. Pour in the wine, bring to the boil, then turn the heat down to low.

Add the grapes and continue cooking gently to warm through – about
2 minutes. Put the mixture onto the toast and sprinkle with the parsley.

Health note This dish is
particularly beneficial for women.
It's a wonderful source of iron and
vitamin B12, the vital ingredients to
prevent anaemia and make healthy
blood. During their child-bearing
years, most women hover on the
borderline of anaemia and are likely
to have very low stores of iron.

Chicken liver pâté with pistachio nuts

Serves 4

2 tablespoons olive oil

1 medium onion, finely chopped

*275g (10oz) chicken livers
(defrosted frozen livers will do),
all membranes removed*

2 hard-boiled eggs, peeled

*2 tablespoons pistachio nuts,
roughly crushed*

The use of nuts and nut oils is common in all Sephardi cooking, and in Mediterranean areas olive oil is an every-day staple. Pistachios, although grown throughout the Mediterranean, were a particular favourite of the Persian Jews; in fact, the name comes from *pistakion*, the ancient Greek corruption of the Persian word *pistah*.

Method Heat the oil in a frying pan, add the onion and sauté gently until soft. Meanwhile, grill the chicken livers until well done. Mix the livers with the onion in the pan, then put the frying-pan contents (including the oil) into a blender or food-processor. Add the eggs and whizz until smooth.

Tip into a bowl, add the pistachio nuts and mix gently but well. Spoon the pâté into a small, attractive dish, smooth the top and chill for at least 3 hours.

Health note This version of chicken liver pâté is rich in protein, iron and B vitamins from the liver. Thanks to the oil and nuts, it also contains substantial amounts of monounsaturated fats, which help reduce cholesterol levels, a benefit aided and abetted by the onion.

Sweet salami salad

Serves 6–8

*175g (6oz) rice (preferably a
mixture of white and wild),
cooked*

*150g (5oz) fresh or defrosted
frozen sweetcorn*

2 spring onions, finely chopped

1 pickled cucumber, rinsed and diced

75g (3oz) lowish-fat salami, diced

For the dressing

*150ml (1/4 pint) extra-virgin
olive oil*

50ml (2fl oz) white wine vinegar

*1 strong spring onion, very finely
chopped*

2 pinches of dry mustard

*1/2 teaspoon organic brown caster
sugar*

Kosher salami is usually made from beef, though veal is sometimes used. It's nearly always flavoured with garlic, although in Latin America they use chilli, while eastern Europe favours paprika. In Holland, they eat an unusual salami that isn't cooked or smoked, but more like steak tartare in a sausage skin. One of my favourites is a beef and garlic salami which has been smoked, then air-dried.

This is typical foodstuff of the Jews from Italy and the mountain regions of Germany and Switzerland. As it's a fairly hard salami, you can slice it very thinly and it tends to have less fat than its non-Kosher equivalents.

Method Mix the salad ingredients together in a bowl.

Put all the dressing ingredients into a large jug and whisk well. Pour the dressing over the salad to serve.

Kiddush cup   This cup would have been used for the blessing over wine at the Sabbath and at the beginning of every festival. There are two scenes from the life of Abraham embossed on the coconut goblet: the three angels visiting Abraham to announce the birth of Isaac (centre left), the binding of Isaac (far right). There is also a scene from the life of Joseph: men drinking (far left). The stem and base (see also page 160) are made from rosewood and the cup was made in England in 1803. It is very likely that the man who commissioned it would have been called Abraham.

soups

Lemon and egg

Serves 6

*1.8 litres (3 pints) chicken stock,
  preferably home-made - see
  recipe for Chicken soup with
  matzo dumplings (page 66)
  or use a good-quality, low-salt
  cube or bouillon powder such as
  Kallo or Marigold*
175g (6oz) long-grain rice
4 egg yolks
1 heaped tablespoon flour
Juice of 3 lemons
1 tablespoon finely chopped parsley

There have been Jews in Greece since classical times. Although, tragically, virtually the whole community was wiped out in the latter stages of the Second World War, they had been masters of adapting the Jewish dietary laws to the traditional regional food of their adopted country.

This light, nourishing and easily digestible broth was a favourite recipe used when breaking the fast of Yom Kippur (the Day of Atonement).

Method Bring the stock to the boil, add the rice and cook until just tender – about 12 minutes.

Meanwhile, cream the egg yolks and beat in the flour. Add the lemon juice and heat in a basin resting over a pan of gently simmering water, stirring continuously, until it just starts to thicken. Gradually add some of the stock, a tablespoon at a time, continuing to stir until you have a thin paste. Pour into the stock and rice and heat gently, being careful not to let it boil.

Season to taste and serve sprinkled with parsley.

Spinach with yogurt

Serves 4

25g (1oz) unsalted butter
*1 large garlic clove, very finely
  chopped*
225g (8oz) baby spinach
*1 tablespoon fresh mint, finely
  chopped*
*900ml (about 1½ pints) live
  natural yogurt*
1 teaspoon crushed caraway seeds
Paprika, to serve
4 small sprigs of mint, to serve

One of the great joys of Greek food is the variety of regional cooking with its subtle local influences. It's not surprising, then, that the dishes of Greek Jews reflect this wonderful diverse cuisine.

This soup, from Crete, includes the universal Greek favourites, spinach and yogurt, with added paprika as an indication of its Ottoman origins.

Method Put the butter into a large saucepan. Add the garlic and sauté gently for 2 minutes.

Wash the spinach thoroughly and add to the pan with only the water still clinging to it. Add the mint. Cover and steam slowly, shaking the pan every 30 seconds or so, until the spinach is wilted – about 5 minutes.

Put the yogurt into another pan with the caraway seeds. Heat through, but don't boil. Add the spinach and its juices and stir well.

Serve sprinkled sparingly with paprika and decorated with mint sprigs.

Barley with mushrooms and marjoram

Serves 4-6

For the stock

You can use good-quality, low-salt
Kosher vegetable stock cubes or
bouillon powder, but this home-
made stock is infinitely better.

2 onions, 1 quartered, 1 left whole

2 large carrots, cut into large chunks

1 fennel bulb, quartered

1 large leek, cut into large chunks

1 turnip, quartered

4 large mushrooms, quartered

2 celery sticks, cut into large chunks

6 bay leaves

1 large sprig of sage

2 sprigs of thyme

1 sprig of rosemary

10 black peppercorns

For the soup

*3 tablespoons sunflower or
  rapeseed oil*

*2 leeks, white parts only, finely
  chopped*

1 garlic clove, finely chopped

*110g (4oz) pearl barley, thoroughly
  washed*

2 bay leaves

*1 litre (1³/4 pints) vegetable stock
  (see above)*

1 carrot, finely diced

*110g (4oz) mushrooms, with stalks,
  finely diced*

*4 large sprigs of fresh marjoram
  (or oregano) or 1 level teaspoon
  either dried herb*

300ml (1/2 pint) sour cream

1 small bunch of chives, snipped

My mother's eldest sister, Ada, was married to a taciturn, fierce Polish tailor whose heavily accented English was difficult to understand – especially for my cousins and me as we were growing up. They lived in Willesden, north London, in a house filled with dark, heavy furniture and thick curtains that always used to be closed. It was one of the few places where the family gathered where the children had to sit quietly and be on their best behaviour for fear of upsetting Uncle Henry. Ada was a wonderful cook and we nearly always had this soup: a traditional Ashkenazi Polish recipe. Henry always complained that it never tasted like his mother's version. But I loved it then and you'll love it now.

Method First, make the stock by putting all the stock ingredients in a large saucepan. Add about 1.5 litres (2¹/2 pints) water. Bring to the boil and simmer, uncovered, for 1 hour. Strain, pushing the vegetable pulp through the sieve with a wooden spoon.

To make the soup, melt the oil in a large pan and gently sauté the leeks and garlic until soft but not brown. Add the barley, bay leaves and stock, and simmer until the barley is tender – about 40 minutes. Add the carrot, mushrooms and marjoram (or oregano) and simmer until the carrots are tender. Discard the bay leaves and any woody herb stalks. Season and stir in the sour cream, reserving one spoonful for each bowl to be used as a topping.

Serve with a blob of sour cream and the chives scattered on top.

Ajo blanco

I'm not sure whether I was more impressed by the synagogue or this amazing soup the first time I visited Cadíz, in southern Spain, with my very dear friend John Belmont – sadly, no longer with us. Fleeing the Nazi occupation of Belgium as a young boy, John had walked his way through Europe; he managed to get to Spain and finally settled in London. He spoke several languages, was a wonderful raconteur and had an uncanny Jewish nose for good food. After seeing the synagogue, he sniffed out a tiny side-street café and insisted that we started with this soup.

Imagine my surprise when what I assumed were black olives floating on the top turned out to be sweet grapes, which contrasted wonderfully with the sharp flavour of garlic. Thanks to the garlic, this is heart protection in a bowl.

Method Mix together the oil, garlic and almonds. Put into a blender with half the breadcrumbs, half the grape juice and 250ml (9fl oz) water. Whizz until smooth and pour into a large bowl.

Put the remainder of the grape juice and the breadcrumbs, the yogurt and another 250ml (9fl oz) water into the blender and whizz until smooth. Combine the two mixtures, stir well and chill.

Serve with the grapes on the side or floating on top.

Serves 6

3 tablespoons extra-virgin olive oil

8 large garlic cloves, very finely chopped

225g (8oz) ground almonds

150g (5oz) fresh white breadcrumbs

500ml (18fl oz) white grape juice

200ml (7fl oz) live natural yogurt

16 seedless black grapes, halved

Sweet and sour tomatoes with noodles

Serves 4

6 large tomatoes

2 tablespoons tomato purée

Juice of 1 medium lemon

2 tablespoons demerara sugar

*1.2 litres (2 pints) chicken stock,
preferably home-made – see
recipe for Chicken soup with
matzo dumplings (page 66)
or use a good-quality, low-salt
cube or bouillon powder such as
Kallo or Marigold*

75g (3oz) rice noodles

In parts of the Middle East, such as ancient Persia, Morocco and Iraq, as well as in the Far East and China, Jews developed a taste for sweet-and-sour dishes. These have become a hallmark of much Sephardi cooking.

All soups really do taste better when prepared with home-made stock, but it's particularly worth the extra effort for this delicately flavoured dish. Of course, you can make it with vegetable stock (see recipe for Barley with mushrooms and marjoram on page 47) if you're planning it as part of a non-meat meal.

Method Put the tomatoes into a blender and whizz until completely broken down. Put them in a large pan with the tomato purée, lemon juice, sugar and stock. Simmer for 25 minutes.

Add the noodles and continue simmering until the noodles are cooked – usually about 5 minutes, but check the packet instructions. Check the seasoning and serve.

Health note This soup is exceptionally rich in the important carotenoid lycopene (in the tomatoes and tomato purée), which is specifically protective against prostate cancer, breast cancer and eye problems.

Potato soup

Serves 4-6

4 tablespoons olive oil

*450g (1lb) old potatoes, peeled
   and diced*

2 large carrots, peeled and diced

1 medium onion, very finely sliced

1 garlic clove, very finely chopped

About 250ml (9fl oz) milk

1 teaspoon ground fennel seeds

*900ml (1^1/$_2$ pints) live
   natural yogurt*

4 sprigs of dill, to garnish

Greek cooking had its own classical origins, but was heavily influenced by the neighbouring Balkans, Turks and the many nations with which the Greeks traded. Jews settling in Greece borrowed from all these cooking styles.

Method Heat the oil in a large pan and gently sauté the potatoes, carrots, onion and garlic until soft but not brown – about 10 minutes. Add just enough milk to cover and simmer until soft – about 15 minutes. Mix the fennel seeds with the yogurt and heat gently in another pan, being careful not to allow it to boil. Tip the vegetables into the yogurt mixture and warm through.

   If you want a smooth soup, liquidise and warm through again. Serve with the dill sprigs on top.

Health note This soup is a good source of energy, and is low in fat and rich in carotenoids from the carrots. It also contains heart-protective phytochemicals from the onions and garlic, and lots of calcium from the milk and yogurt. The fennel seeds improve digestion and ensure that you get the most out of every spoonful.

Cream of jerusalem artichoke

Serves 4

*1 skinless chicken breast, cut into
   strands along the grain of the
   meat*

2 tablespoons olive oil

450g (1lb) Jerusalem artichokes

*1 litre (1^3/4 pints) chicken stock,
   preferably home-made – see
   recipe for Chicken soup with
   matzo dumplings (page 66)
   or use a good-quality, low-salt
   cube or bouillon powder such as
   Kallo or Marigold*

*4 tablespoons finely chopped
   flat-leaf parsley*

Jerusalem artichokes have nothing to do with Jerusalem. Their name is a corruption of the Italian word *girasole*, which means 'sunflower', to which these delicious little tubers are related. In this soup, their unique flavour is combined with protein, and vitamin-rich chicken to make a nourishing and unusual soup that is just as good cold as hot.

Method Stir-fry the chicken pieces in the olive oil and reserve. Simmer the Jerusalem artichokes in the stock until tender – about 15 minutes. Whizz in a blender or food-processor until smooth. Put back into a large saucepan, add the chicken and reheat gently.

   Serve scattered with parsley.

Health note Jerusalem artichokes are rich in inulin, which isn't broken down during digestion and ends up in the large bowel, where it provides food for the beneficial probiotic bacteria.

White beans with pasta and chard

Serves 6-8

5 tablespoons olive oil

1 small onion, finely chopped

2 garlic cloves, finely chopped

1 carrot, finely diced

1 stick celery, finely sliced

*225g (8oz) chard or rainbow chard,
    leaves separated from the stalks,
    but both reserved*

*1.8 litres (3 pints) vegetable stock –
    see recipe for Barley with
    mushrooms and marjoram
    (page 47) or use a good-quality,
    low-salt cube or bouillon powder
    such as Kallo or Marigold*

*350g (12oz) canned cannellini,
    butter or other white bean
    (drained weight), rinsed and
    drained*

*250g (9oz) small pasta such as
    fusilli or farfalle (or farfel: small,
    grain-like pieces of toasted pasta)*

*About 6 tablespoons grated
    Parmesan cheese*

This is a Kosher adaptation of the great Italian peasant soup, *pasta e fagioli*, and it's closer to the Naples version, which is made with olive oil instead of the butter and pancetta used in other parts of Italy. You can always omit the Parmesan if you're serving this as part of a meat meal.

With lots of protein and heart-protective natural chemicals in the beans, and the amazing content of beta-carotene and other vital carotenoids in the chard, this soup is a substantial and nourishing meal on its own.

Method Put the oil into a large pan and gently sauté the onion, garlic, carrot, celery and chard stalks for about 10 minutes. Add the stock and bring to the boil. Add the beans to the soup and bring back to the boil. After 2 minutes, add the torn green chard leaves and cook for another 3–4 minutes until the beans are tender. Keep warm.

Cook the pasta according to the packet instructions. Drain and add to the bean mixture. Serve scattered with Parmesan cheese.

Tomatoes with peppers

Serves 4

8 large spring onions, finely
  chopped

2 garlic cloves, finely chopped

3 tablespoons olive oil

4 large red peppers, deseeded and
  finely chopped

2 large tomatoes, roughly chopped

1 litre (1 3/4 pints) vegetable stock –
  see recipe for Barley with
  mushrooms and marjoram
  (page 47) or use a good-quality,
  low-salt cube or bouillon powder
  such as Kallo or Marigold

2 large sprigs of thyme

1 large sprig of rosemary

There doesn't seem to be any evidence of Jews in South America until the 16th century, so it's unlikely that any Jewish cook came into contact with tomatoes before then. Tomatoes were first introduced to Europe by the Spanish in the 1700s, and they soon spread throughout the Mediterranean into north Africa and the Middle East. As members of the nightshade family of plants, they weren't popular to begin with – people were afraid to eat them because of their deadly relative. But it wasn't long before they were embraced by all cooks – Jewish, Muslim and Christian.

Method Gently sauté the onions and garlic in the oil until softened but not brown. Add the peppers and tomatoes and continue to cook for 5 minutes, stirring continuously. Add the stock and herbs, bring to the boil and simmer until the peppers are tender – about 10 minutes.

Remove the woody herb stalks and whizz the soup in a blender or food-processor until smooth. Serve hot or chilled.

Health note Combined here in the Mediterranean favourites of garlic, peppers, thyme and rosemary, the health benefits of this dish are powerfully protective and nourishing – but you'll enjoy it simply for its taste.

Quick borscht

Serves 4-6

900g (2lb) fresh beetroot, peeled
* and diced*
1 medium turnip, diced
2 celery sticks, roughly chopped
2 garlic cloves
2 carrots, roughly chopped
3 tablespoons olive oil
1 litre (1 3/4 pints) vegetable stock –
* see recipe for Barley with*
* mushrooms and marjoram*
* (page 47) or use a good-quality,*
* low-salt cube or bouillon powder*
* such as Kallo or Marigold*
250ml (9fl oz) live natural yogurt
Juice of 1 lemon

Beetroot is one of the greatest of health-giving vegetables. It was revered by the ancient Greeks, used by the Romanies as a blood-building medicine, and is given to convalescent patients in Russia, Poland and most of eastern Europe to this day. In traditional medicine, beetroot has been used as a treatment for leukaemia and anaemia, and modern science has discovered specific anticarcinogens in this vegetable's red colouring.

Not all of the Ashkenazi cooking from eastern Europe is instant heart attack on a plate, and this recipe is not only delicious (hot or cold), but a provider of great nutritional benefits too. My mother always served this with sour cream, but yogurt contains far less fat. If she wanted to serve borscht with a meat meal, she would leave out the sour cream and thicken it with beaten egg yolk. I prefer to use soya yogurt.

Method Put the beetroot, turnip, celery, garlic and carrots into a food-processor and whizz them finely.

Put the oil into a large pan and gently sauté the vegetables, stirring continuously, for 5 minutes. Pour in the stock and simmer for 30 minutes. Strain into a clean saucepan and bring back to a simmer.

Mix the yogurt and lemon juice well. Serve the soup in individual bowls with a swirl of yogurt sauce on top.

Courgette soup with dolcelatte

1 onion, finely chopped

1 leek, finely chopped

3 tablespoons olive oil

4 courgettes, finely sliced

600ml (1 pint) vegetable stock –
see recipe for Barley with
mushrooms and marjoram
(page 47) or use a good-quality,
low-salt cube or bouillon powder
such as Kallo or Marigold

450ml (16fl oz) semi-skimmed milk

200g (7oz) dolcelatte cheese

When I was growing up in the small Hertfordshire town of Tring, nearly all my schoolfriends were Christian. It wasn't many years before I tasted the traditional Christmas leftover favourite, Brussels sprouts and Stilton soup. When I was a student living in London, I met a Jewish girl whose family had been expelled from Egypt. Her mother was Italian, and imagine my surprise when, invited to eat with them, she served this wonderful soup which she said was her grandmother's recipe from Rome! The taste took me instantly back to my childhood in Tring and reminded me, even then, that food is a great way to build bridges between people.

Method Gently sauté the onion and leek in the oil until soft but not brown. Add the courgettes, stock and milk. Bring to the boil and simmer very gently until the courgettes are tender – about 10 minutes.

Whizz in a blender or food-processor until smooth. Return to the saucepan and bring back to a simmer. Crumble in the cheese and stir until dissolved.

Health note Leeks, like onions and garlic, help to lower cholesterol and protect against infection, the skin of courgettes is rich in beta-carotene, and the milk and cheese provide protein and lots of calcium for strong bones.

Avocado cream

6 spring onions, very finely
chopped

1 garlic clove, very finely chopped

3 tablespoons olive oil

2 heaped tablespoons flour

1 litre (1³/4 pints) semi-skimmed
milk

1 large or 2 small ripe avocados

1 egg yolk

100ml (3¹/2fl oz) live natural yogurt

4 tablespoons snipped chives

For 8,000 years, the indigenous peoples of South America have eaten avocados and used the rest of the tree – leaves, rind, seeds and bark – as medicines. Israel is one of the world's major growers of avocados, and this delicious soup is a great way to enjoy their benefits.

Method Gently sauté the onions and garlic in the olive oil until softened but not brown. Take off the heat and sprinkle in the flour, stirring continuously. Return to the heat and cook gently until well combined and thickened. Still stirring, gradually add the milk.

Mash the avocado(s) and add to the pan immediately. Heat through, stirring continuously. Mix together the egg yolk and yogurt and add to the pan. Warm through gently; don't allow it to boil.

Serve warm with the chives scattered on top.

Health note This is a super-nutrient food, rich in mono-unsaturated fats to reduce cholesterol and with significant amounts of oleic acid, an antioxidant that protects against some cancers, strokes and heart disease.

Summer berries

Serves 4

900g (2lb) mixed summer berries
Juice of 1/2 lemon
1 tablespoon runny honey
1 teaspoon ground cinnamon
1 heaped teaspoon arrowroot
4 tablespoons live natural yogurt

Here's another fruit soup which has been traditionally eaten for generations in eastern Europe, especially in Hungary, where they grow wonderful summer berries. Although cooked, the fruit will still provide good amounts of vitamin C as there's so much there to start with.

Method Put the fruit, lemon juice, honey and cinnamon into a large pan with 700ml (1¼ pints) water. Simmer until the fruit is soft. Push through a sieve with a wooden spoon and return to the pan.

Mix the arrowroot with a little water to make a firm paste. Add to the pan and bring slowly to the boil, stirring continuously.

Serve cold, with a spoonful of yogurt in each bowl. (Omit the yogurt if serving as part of a meat meal.)

Health note All the dark berries are among the richest sources of the protective ORAC antioxidant units (see page 13). As a bonus, the most recent research shows that cinnamon can help regulate blood-sugar levels and prevent type-2 diabetes.

Red grapes with nuts

Serves 4

225g (8oz) red grapes

450ml (16fl oz) live natural yogurt

600ml (1 pint) semi-skimmed milk

2 tablespoons runny honey

4 tablespoons ground walnuts

Grated zest of 1 lemon

1 teaspoon vanilla extract

8 walnut halves

Chilled fruit soups are an enormous source of vitamin C as they're often uncooked, so none of this nutrient is lost. Most Jewish cookbooks include at least one fruit soup, and they're a traditional favourite in eastern Europe, Russia, Germany and Israel. Melon soup is popular in Russia, red cherry in Hungary, and every imaginable fruit soup is to be found in Israel.

Although wine is an integral part of Jewish religious practice, alcohol has never featured largely in Jewish social life. Historically, I think these soups were used in place of bitter aperitifs as an appetite stimulant.

Method   Push the grapes through a sieve with a wooden spoon.

Whisk the yogurt, milk and honey together and mix in the grape pulp. Stir in the ground walnuts, lemon zest and vanilla extract. Serve chilled with the walnut halves floating on top.

Health note   In this recipe, there are all the protective properties of the antioxidants in grapes combined with the cholesterol-lowering monounsaturated fats in the walnuts.

Asian cod and chickpea soup

Serves 4

4 plum tomatoes

2 large red peppers

About 5 tablespoons olive oil

4 shallots, each cut into 8 pieces

2 garlic cloves, finely chopped

1 small fennel bulb, finely sliced

*2 red chillies, deseeded and finely
  sliced*

1 teaspoon ground turmeric

$1/2$ teaspoon ground cumin

*1 litre ($1^3/4$ pints) fish or vegetable
  stock*

275g (10oz) cod fillet, in small pieces

*250g (9oz), drained weight, canned
  chickpeas, drained and rinsed*

*3 tablespoons finely chopped
  mixed parsley, coriander and mint*

Juice of 1 small lemon

My mother used to make fish soup, but refused to use the eels which my Dutch father said were acceptable to most Dutch Jews. Nice though her version was, it was also a bit weak and feeble. If only she'd known an Asian Jewish family, her fish soup would have been like this hot, spicy and substantial dish! Full of protein, fibre and protective antioxidants, it is a health feast as well as a taste delight.

Method   Preheat the oven to 220°C/425°F/gas mark 7. Roast the tomatoes and peppers for about 30 minutes, until charred. When they're cool enough to handle, rub the skins off the peppers, deseed and cut into strips. Quarter the tomatoes.

Put the oil into a large saucepan and gently sauté the shallots and garlic for 3 minutes. Add the fennel and chillies and continue cooking for another 3 minutes. Sprinkle in the turmeric and cumin. Stir well and cook for 2 minutes. Add the stock and bring to a simmer. Tip in the fish, chickpeas, peppers, tomatoes and 2 tablespoons of the herbs, and continue simmering gently until the fish is cooked – about 10 minutes.

Sprinkle with the lemon juice, scatter with the remaining herbs and serve.

Fish with watercress

Serves 6

For the stock

You can use good-quality, low-salt
Kosher fish stock cubes or fish
or vegetable bouillon powder,
but this home-made stock is
infinitely better.

110g (4oz) fish trimmings and bones

3 carrots, roughly chopped

2 white onions, roughly chopped

1 leek, roughly chopped

1 sprig of rosemary

6 large sprigs of parsley

1 large sprig of mint

3 large sprigs of tarragon

8 white peppercorns

1/2 teaspoon salt

For the soup

500g (18oz) firm white-fish fillets
  (e.g. cod, halibut, haddock), cut
  into very fine goujons along the
  grain of the flesh

1/2 teaspoon sea salt

1/2 teaspoon ginger paste

4 tablespoons sherry

1.5 litres (2 1/2 pints) fish stock (see
  above)

3 teaspoons light soy sauce

1 teaspoon demerara sugar

2 large bunches watercress, leaves
  stripped from the stalks

6 spring onions, trimmed and cut
  diagonally

Here's another sweet-and-sour recipe, this time from the Far East. My cousin Ann trained as a nurse in London and went to work in America, where she met her future husband. Ira, a psychologist with the American military, was posted to the Far East, where they got married, and Ann sent me this recipe from a friend she met through the local rabbi.

Serve with rice cakes and a mixed salad and you have a perfect light lunch or supper.

Method To make the stock, put all the ingredients into a large saucepan and add 2 litres (3 1/2 pints) water. Bring to the boil and simmer for 30 minutes. Strain through a sieve or kitchen muslin.

To make the soup, sprinkle the fish with sea salt. Mix the ginger paste with half the sherry, pour over the fish and leave to marinate for about 30 minutes.

Bring the stock to the boil and add the soy sauce, sugar and the remainder of the sherry. Put the watercress leaves into a large bowl, with the fish on top. Ensuring that the stock is still boiling, pour it into the bowl and leave for 10 minutes. Serve scattered with the spring onions.

Health note With absolutely no fat, lots of protein, iodine and other minerals from the fish, huge cancer-fighting benefits from the watercress and the energising stimulation from the ginger, this soup is exceptionally healthy.

Smoked haddock and smoked salmon

Serves 4

50g (2oz) unsalted butter

1 onion, finely chopped

600ml (1 pint) semi-skimmed milk

3 bay leaves

1/2 teaspoon ground nutmeg

275g (10oz) potatoes, cut into 1cm
 (1/2in) dice

350g (12oz) undyed smoked
 haddock, skin removed and
 broken along the grain into
 bite-sized pieces

200ml (7fl oz) low-fat crème
 fraîche or double cream

110g (4oz) smoked salmon, cut into
 batons

Black pepper

Dill fronds, to serve

British Jews were no different from those who spread to the far-flung corners of the earth as they also adapted their food to available ingredients. I discovered how regional these adaptations were when staying with a Jewish family in Glasgow who were friends of my parents.

I was expecting smoked salmon, but not this wonderful variation of the traditional Scottish cullen skink. It is healthier made with low-fat crème fraîche, but forty years ago there was no alternative to the double cream that made it so unashamedly rich. I've persuaded myself that the benefits of oily fish and the total lack of fat in the haddock balance out the cream. My wife still makes it; sometimes we're very good, sometimes we aren't.

Method Melt the butter in a large saucepan and gently sauté the onion until soft but not brown. Pour in the milk, add the bay leaves, nutmeg and potatoes and simmer until the potatoes are just starting to become tender – about 10 minutes. Add the smoked haddock and simmer until cooked – about 7 minutes. Lift out the fish. Remove and discard the bay leaves.

Mash the potatoes thoroughly. Return the fish and add the crème fraîche or cream. Season to taste with pepper. Bring quickly to the boil, take off the heat and add the smoked salmon.

Serve hot with the dill fronds floating on top.

Spiced lamb soup

Serves 8

For the stock
You can use good-quality, low-salt Kosher lamb stock cubes or bouillon powder, but this home-made stock is infinitely better.

900g (2lb) lamb bones, sawn into 4cm (1½in) pieces

2 large red onions, coarsely chopped

2 large carrots, coarsely chopped

1 leek, coarsely chopped

2 celery sticks, coarsely chopped

1 large bunch of sage

1 sprig of rosemary

5 bay leaves

10 black peppercorns

For the soup
700g (1½lb) stewing lamb, cubed

2 litres (3½ pints) lamb stock (see above)

2 medium courgettes, cut into thick slices

2 heaped tablespoons tomato purée

6 shallots, quartered

3 garlic cloves, finely chopped

½ teaspoon ground turmeric

½ teaspoon caraway seeds

1 saffron strand

Isolated and cut off from the rest of world's Jewry for 2,000 years, the Jews of Ethiopia are an extraordinary people. Unaffected by the rabbinical interpretations of the laws of Kosher cooking, theirs is a style of food that is probably much closer to that of the biblical Jews than anything we eat today. Surviving as they did in the harsh climate of Ethiopia and often in difficult circumstances, to them meat was probably a luxury; when they had it, nothing was wasted. Like the Indians, Ethiopian Jews used pieces of large, flat bread to pick up their food. Also like the Indians, they had a taste for hot spices.

This recipe calls for lamb stock, but exactly the same method can be used to make beef stock, which also features in many of the recipes in this book.

Method First, make the stock. Preheat the oven to 220°C/425°F/gas mark 7. Roast the bones for 30 minutes. Then put them, together with any meat still left clinging, into a large saucepan. Add the remainder of the stock ingredients and 3 litres (5 pints) water. Bring to the boil and simmer for 4 hours, regularly skimming off any fat. Sieve or strain through muslin. Cover, leave until cold and remove any remaining fat.

To make the soup, put all ingredients into a large saucepan. Bring to the boil and simmer for 2 hours, regularly skimming off any fat.

Health note This soup is a westernised adaptation of a traditional nourishing and sustaining dish, with the added protection against stomach cancer provided by the turmeric.

Lentils with meatballs

Serves 4

*350g (12oz) green lentils, rinsed
and soaked in cold water for at
least 2 hours (or according to the
packet instructions)*

2 small onions, very finely chopped

2 garlic cloves, very finely chopped

*1 small fennel bulb, very finely
chopped*

2 carrots, finely diced

2 large tomatoes, coarsely chopped

2 tablespoons tomato purée

1 large sprig of rosemary

1 large sprig of thyme

2 bay leaves

*350g (12oz) best-quality (i.e. with
less fat) minced beef or lamb*

Olive oil

*4 tablespoons chopped flat-leaf
parsley*

In many parts of the world, and at different times in their history, Jewish communities prospered. But to me they seem never to have lost the survival instincts which come from their history of travelling the wilderness, enslavement, bondage and persecution. This made their women frugal cooks who helped their families survive on the most meagre of resources.

In terms of nutritional value for money, there's little to compare with lentils and all their relatives, and the Jewish housewives adapted them, whether they were making *dhal* in India, Kurdish dishes in Iraq or soups and stews throughout the Mediterranean. Jews certainly ate lentils in ancient Rome, where their Latin name was *lenticula*, and in medieval France, where they were known as *lentilles*. Although the green *lentilles du Puy* may be the gourmet's choice, green lentils are also produced in Umbria in southern Italy, where this soup still makes a substantial and popular meal.

Method Put the lentils, onions, garlic, fennel, carrots, tomatoes, tomato purée, rosemary, thyme and bay leaves into a large pan. Pour in 1.5 litres (2^1/2 pints) water. Bring to the boil and simmer until the lentils are starting to become tender – about 15-20 minutes.

While they're cooking, season the meat and roll into balls about the size of walnuts. Heat the oil in a large pan and fry the meatballs until they're brown all over. Remove the bay leaves and the woody stems of the rosemary and thyme from the lentil mixture.

Add the meatballs to the lentils and simmer until both lentils and meatballs are cooked – about 25 minutes. Serve scattered with the chopped parsley.

Chicken with matzo dumplings *(knaidlach)*

Serves 4-6

For the stock

You can use good-quality, low-salt Kosher chicken stock cubes or bouillon powder, but this home-made stock is infinitely better.

1 leftover chicken carcass, all skin and fat removed

2 Spanish onions, 1 whole and unpeeled, the other peeled and chopped

1 leek, coarsely chopped

3 celery sticks, with leaves if possible, coarsely chopped

4 bay leaves

1 large sprig of rosemary

2 large sprigs of thyme

1 large sprig of sage

4 large sprigs of parsley

12 white peppercorns

For the dumplings *(knaidlach)*

200g (7oz) medium matzo meal

3 eggs

1 tablespoon olive oil

1 tablespoon finely chopped flat leaf parsley

3 grindings of black pepper

2 pinches of salt

This recipe makes a clear broth, but if you wish to turn it into a concentrated chicken stock, continue simmering until the volume is reduced by half. It can then be strained and frozen and used in many of the other recipes in this book. Of course, you can remove the carcass and the unpeeled onion, return any remaining chicken meat to the pot and serve as a more substantial chicken and vegetable soup, omitting the dumplings (*knaidlach*).

If you don't have a chicken carcass, boil a whole chicken for the soup and use the meat in other dishes, such as Greek chicken patties (see page 42). Traditionally, a boiling fowl from a Kosher butcher would be used.

Method First, make the stock. Put the carcass in a large pan and cover with about 2.4 litres (4 pints) water. Bring to the boil, cover and simmer for 30 minutes. Add the vegetables, herbs and peppercorns, bring back to the boil, cover and simmer for 1 hour. Strain, reserving the stock.

Make the dumplings by mixing all the dumpling ingredients together, then knead until you have a smooth dough, adding a little water if necessary. Cover and leave to rest for at least 3 hours.

Using your hands, form the mixture into balls the size of apricots.

To put it all together, bring the chicken stock up to simmering point. Drop in the dumplings and continue simmering, covered, for 30 minutes.

Health note This is the famous 'Jewish penicillin' beloved of every mother and grandmother. It's not an old wives' tale; there's good scientific evidence that it contains vitamins, minerals and other natural chemicals that are antibacterial and immune-boosting. In addition, nutrients and valuable plant chemicals are extracted from the vegetables and herbs during the cooking process, most of which end up as active ingredients in the finished soup.

Glass flask This beautifully proportioned 19th-century flask was used on the Sabbath for oil, or more probably wine, and is engraved with verses from the Bible that formed part of the Kiddush blessing. The inscription on the neck is a decorative Arabic script that is apparently meaningless. It is thought that the bottle was made in Syria by Mordecai Shiqfaati, but its round base means that it cannot stand up unsupported – not the most practical design for a household object.

vegetables and salads

Red cabbage with apples and caraway

Serves 4

*1 medium red cabbage, finely
    shredded*
1 tablespoon cider vinegar
1 teaspoon caraway seeds
2 tablespoons demerara sugar
*2 large cooking apples, peeled,
    cored and quartered*

Cabbage was one of the few vegetables available to Ashkenazi Jews in the harsh climate of eastern Europe. In western Europe, although a large range of produce was readily available, cabbage remained a firm favourite.

Caraway is native to India, Asia and parts of southern Europe and gets its name from the Arabic *al-karawiya* ('the cumin'), which was used as medicine by the ancient Egyptians. In fact, fossilised seeds have been excavated from sites 5,000 years old, and they have also been found where caravans followed the Silk Route. By the time Shakespeare mentioned caraway in *Henry IV*, it was already a popular flavouring in Germany and England. This typically German recipe uses the seed not only to flavour the cabbage, but also to reduce the dish's 'flatulence factor'.

Delicious hot or cold, this dish goes well with cold meat, fish and other salads.

Method Put the cabbage, vinegar, caraway seeds and sugar into a large saucepan. Add 125ml (4fl oz) water and bring to the boil. Put the apples on top, cover the pan and simmer gently until the cabbage is tender and the apples are mushy – about 40 minutes.

Remove carefully to a serving dish, trying to leave most of the apples on top of the cabbage.

Health note Long regarded as 'the medicine of the poor', all cabbage provides exceptional health benefits: protection from cancer, improved digestive function, an abundance of vitamin C and folic acid and, in the red cabbage used here, substantial quantities of beta-carotene.

Spiced leeks

Serves 4

About 450ml (16fl oz) vegetable
  stock – see recipe for Barley with
  mushrooms and marjoram
  (page 47) or use a good-quality,
  low-salt cube or bouillon powder
  such as Kallo or Marigold
2 bay leaves, broken in half across
  the spines
1 teaspoon coriander seeds
1 teaspoon caraway seeds
8 small leeks, cleaned and trimmed
  but left whole
4 tablespoons olive oil

Leeks grew wild in biblical times and were very popular with the ancient Hebrews. They've remained so ever since in both Sephardic and Ashkenazi communities. Because cultivated leeks thrive in cold climates as well as they do in the Mediterranean (in fact, they taste much better after a touch of frost), they were a common addition to soups, stews and casseroles.

Served here as a vegetable in their own right, they have all the cardio-protective benefits of their relatives onions and garlic, and also help in the relief of coughs and colds. In ancient Rome, they were specially cultivated on the orders of Nero, who ate leeks every day to improve his voice. I don't know if it was wandering Jews who introduced them to the Welsh, but it's possible...

Method Bring the stock to the boil. Add the bay leaves, coriander and caraway seeds and boil briskly for 1 minute.

Put the leeks into a flameproof casserole and pour over the stock and olive oil. Cover and simmer (on the hob) until the leeks are tender – about 25 minutes. Put the leeks onto a serving dish and keep warm.

Remove the bay leaves and reduce the cooking liquid by boiling briskly, uncovered, for about 5 minutes. Pour the liquid over the leeks to serve.

Sweet and sour courgettes

Serves 4

4 tablespoons olive oil
8 large courgettes, cut into large
  dice
1 tablespoon finely chopped
  oregano leaves
1 small garlic clove, finely chopped
3 tablespoons red wine vinegar
3 tablespoons demerara sugar
1/2 teaspoon ground cinnamon

Sicilian Jews adopted this Turkish recipe that combines the exotic but typical sweet-and-sour tastes of sugar, vinegar and cinnamon. It's yet another example of how tasty courgettes can be when treated with a little imagination.

Method Warm the oil in a large frying pan and sauté the courgettes, stirring frequently, until softened but not brown.

Using a slotted spoon, put onto a serving plate and scatter with the oregano. Add the garlic, vinegar, sugar, cinnamon and about 2 tablespoons water to the oil remaining in the pan. Bring to the boil and simmer until thickened. Serve the courgettes with the sauce poured on top.

Health note Here we have heart protection from the garlic, beta-carotene from the courgettes and antibacterial phytochemicals from the cinnamon.

Broad beans in olive oil

Serves 4

About 2kg (4½lb) broad beans (unshelled weight), or you could use 1kg (2¼lb) defrosted frozen beans, skinned, if you prefer

About 425ml (¾ pint) vegetable stock – see recipe for Barley with mushrooms and marjoram (page 47) or use a good-quality, low-salt cube or bouillon powder such as Kallo or Marigold

1 large sprig of rosemary

2 tablespoons finely chopped flat leaf parsley

100ml (3½fl oz) extra-virgin olive oil

Black pepper

Broad beans have remained popular in all Jewish communities and they're frequently eaten during Passover as a reminder of Jewish slavery in Egypt, where they formed part of the staple diet. Many broad bean dishes are found in the Sephardic cooking of Greece, Italy and southern France as well as in all Middle Eastern Jewish cuisines.

Also known as fava beans, they are an old Eurasian member of the legume family, and are delicious raw when they're young.

Serve warm or cold, as a vegetable dish or salad.

Method Put the beans into a saucepan and just cover with stock. Add the rosemary, bring to the boil and cook over a high heat, uncovered, until the beans are cooked (about 7 minutes), adding more stock or water if necessary. Remove the rosemary.

Mix the parsley with the olive oil and stir into the beans. Serve scattered with freshly ground black pepper.

Health note Broad beans contain minerals such as iron, zinc, phosphorus and manganese and are also a source of folic acid and vitamin E. They're low in fat, rich in beta-carotene and supply the valuable soluble fibre which helps lower cholesterol levels. They provide good levels of protein and, when eaten together with starchy foods like rice or pasta, they're as good as fillet steak.

Turnips and carrots with garlic

Serves 4

12 garlic cloves, peeled but left
  whole
8 baby turnips, scrubbed, or
  2 older turnips, peeled and diced
8 baby carrots, scrubbed, or
  3 older carrots, peeled and diced
6 tablespoons olive oil
1 sprig of chervil
1 tablespoon runny honey
2 tablespoons finely chopped
  flat-leaf parsley,

Carrots are another favourite in traditional Jewish cooking. Like potatoes and cabbage, they were among the few vegetables which survived the harsh climate of eastern Europe, and were cooked as the traditional dish *tzimmes*: glazed with sugar or honey and always eaten during Rosh Hashanah. Like other sweet dishes eaten during the New Year celebrations, they symbolised a wish that the coming year would be sweet.

Although turnips were popular in parts of the Sephardic world, especially in Iraq, Egypt and Lebanon, where they were mostly eaten as pickles or sweetmeats, they were more widely used by European Jews in stews and casseroles. They have a wonderful ability to absorb juices and flavours, which is why they make such a good accompaniment to fatty dishes like duck and goose. Turnips were particularly popular with Dutch Jews – which is where this recipes originates.

Method Put the garlic into a large saucepan of cold water, bring to the boil and boil for 5 minutes. Drain and set aside.

Put the turnips and carrots into a large pan with half the olive oil, the chervil, honey and just enough water to cover. Simmer, covered, until just tender: about 10–15 minutes. Remove the lid, turn the heat to high and boil off the cooking liquid.

Put the garlic into a very large frying pan and sauté gently in the remainder of the olive oil. Tip the garlic and juices into the turnips and carrots and mix well. Sprinkle with the parsley to serve.

Pomegranate with avocado salad

Serves 4

1 pomegranate

75g (3oz) seedless black grapes,
*   halved*

2 ripe avocados

Special vinaigrette (see page 82)

2 tablespoons freshly chopped
*   mint leaves*

Pomegranates have great significance in Jewish cooking. They originated in Asia, where they grow as a shrub or small tree, and have long been cultivated for their edible fruit, with its tough red outer rind, many seeds and luscious red pulp. They get their name from the Latin words *pomum* and *granatum*, meaning 'apple' and 'full of seeds'.

As children, my cousins and I always looked forward to the festival of Rosh Hashanah, the Jewish New Year: a time when all Jews pray for a year of health, peace and prosperity. All children like sweet things, and this is the time when bread is dipped in honey, followed by slices of apple dipped in honey and the blessing: 'May it be Your will to renew for us a good and sweet year.' It was also the tradition to eat pomegranates, which we did by cutting them in half and picking out the flesh-coloured seeds with a pin. The significance is that our good deeds will be increased like the seeds of the pomegranate. The seeds also signify the desire for many children to be born in the coming year.

Method Halve the pomegranate and use a teaspoon to remove the seeds. Combine with the grapes.

Immediately before serving, halve, peel and stone the avocados and cut into slices. (If you leave avocado pieces sitting on the side, they'll discolour.) Mix together gently with the pomegranates and grapes. Dress with the vinaigrette. Scatter with the mint leaves to serve.

Health note This exotic fruit is full of health-enhancing carotenoids, vitamins and fibre. Avocados are one of the most nutritious of all vegetables (see page 56) and, despite what many people think, they're not fattening.

Olive and orange salad

Jews were the earliest cultivators of citrus fruits. Olives have been cultivated for at least 5,000 years, and they're part of Jewish biblical history. Widely used in Sephardic cuisine, this salad is a favourite in Israel, although its origins are probably north African.

Don't remove all the pith from the oranges as it contains bioflavonoids that protect the walls of blood vessels.

Method Put the oranges into a serving bowl. Scatter the olives over the oranges.

Whisk together the lemon juice, olive oil, garlic, mint, cumin and paprika. Pour the dressing over the salad, adding 2 pinches of paprika to serve.

Health note This recipe combines the taste and vitamin C of oranges with the bitter flavours of olives. Because they're such a good source of oil, olives are often thought to be fattening, but this isn't the case; 18 olives contain only 60 calories, but they provide some vitamin E and lots of protective antioxidants.

Green beans with onion and thyme

Thyme grows wild throughout the southern Mediterranean and was a popular herb with Jewish cooks, whose historical use of culinary herbs can be traced back to the Old Testament. As well as its unmistakable flavour, thyme has many medicinal properties. It was used by the ancient Egyptians for embalming, Greeks burned it in their temples, and Romans used its antiseptic properties for cleaning their houses.

This recipe comes from a tiny Jewish (but not Kosher) restaurant in Nice and is equally delicious cold as part of a salad meal or buffet.

Method Put the onion into a large saucepan and sauté gently in the oil until soft but not brown. Add the beans, thyme and about 200ml (7fl oz) water – just enough to cover the beans.

Cover the pan and cook over a medium heat until the beans are just tender – about 10 minutes. Remove the thyme. Drain the beans and scatter with the chives to serve.

Health note Thyme is a powerful antiseptic and you've probably seen the essential oil thymol extracted from this plant in the pink mouthwash by your dentist's chair.

Beans in garlic

In some parts of the world, Jews are known as 'the garlic- and onion-eaters'. Wandering in the wilderness, Jews remembered the garlic and onions they'd eaten in Egypt (as mentioned in the Book of Numbers, Chapter 11). In fact, the whole allium genus, which also includes shallots, spring onions, chives and leeks, has valuable healing powers.

Method Heat the oil and gently sauté the garlic and spring onions for 3 minutes. Add the tomato purée and mix well. Tip in the beans and add just enough water to cover. Stir in the oregano. Cover and simmer until the beans are just tender – about 10 minutes. Take off the lid and turn the heat to high to reduce the cooking juices – no longer than 2 minutes.

Serve the beans in the juices.

Health note This recipe provides heart-protective, cholesterol-lowering, anticoagulant and blood-pressure-reducing chemicals in abundance. As a bonus, garlic and onions are also helpful for many types of infection, especially coughs and colds. The beans add fibre and beta-carotene.

Opposite: *Green beans with onion and thyme*

Orange beetroot with almonds

The ancient Greeks used beetroot as a medicine and also as offerings to their gods. In eastern Europe, this vibrant red vegetable is valued as a blood strengthener. It is found throughout Europe, North Africa and Asia, and especially in Poland and Russia, where beetroot soup is a national dish.

This recipe combines two favourite Jewish ingredients: beetroot, which has been part of Jewish cuisine since around the 4th century, and almonds, which are mentioned in the Book of Genesis. In both Ashkenazi and Sephardic communities, almonds are a symbolic food on all festive occasions. They are rich in protein, vital minerals and B vitamins and make a perfect companion to the valuable nutrients present in beetroot.

Method Put the beetroot, orange juice, orange zest, if using, and olive oil in a pan and simmer gently for about 10 minutes. Turn up the heat and boil until most of the liquid is reduced.

Meanwhile, dry-fry the almonds until just golden – about 2 minutes. Serve the beetroot in its juice with the almonds scattered on top.

Broad beans with beetroot

Serves 4

225g (8oz) broad beans
  (frozen will do)
4 medium cooked beetroot, diced
About 2 tablespoons extra-virgin
  olive oil
Black pepper

For the magic mayonnaise
(optional)

6 tablespoons of mayonnaise
  (home-made, of course, is best)
  and add one of the following:
1 tablespoon capers, rinsed,
  squeezed dry and chopped
2 gherkins, chopped
2 tablespoons chopped 'soft'
  herbs: chervil, marjoram, basil,
  oregano, etc., not woody herbs
  like rosemary
1 teaspoon Dijon mustard
Mustard and cress, a few chopped
  spring onions or anything else
  that takes your fancy

This is another of my mother's favourite recipes. It combines the beetroot traditions of her own Ashkenazi background with the Sephardic love of broad beans and the Dutch passion for mayonnaise. The beans with mayonnaise came from her Dutch mother-in-law, and she added the beetroot.

A note to orthodox Jews: be wary because some milk by-products may be used in both commercially prepared mayonnaise and ready-made mustard. This is important if you're eating the dish with a meat meal.

Method Cook the broad beans in boiling water until almost tender. Add the beetroot and continue cooking for another 5 minutes. Drain, drizzle with olive oil and serve hot with a few twists of freshly ground black pepper.

Alternatively, serve cold accompanied by the mayonnaise.

Health note Beans and beetroot are exceptionally healthy: good for the blood, circulation, heart and natural resistance. Mayonnaise does, of course, contain some cholesterol, but unless you already have exceptionally high cholesterol levels, it's the cholesterol your body manufactures from saturated animal fat that does the damage – so don't worry about the eggs in the mayonnaise.

Warm onion salad with cucumber and capers

Serves 4

For the special vinaigrette

125ml (4fl oz) extra-virgin olive oil

30ml (1fl oz) walnut oil

30ml (1fl oz) cider vinegar

1/2 teaspoon mustard powder

1/2 teaspoon brown caster sugar

For the salad

2 medium onions, unpeeled

2 tablespoons capers

1/2 cucumber, peeled, deseeded and diced

Onions have been part of Jewish cuisine since ancient Egyptian times; there are biblical references to this delicious and healthy vegetable.

You may think that roasting vegetables is an invention of modern trendy chefs, but Jews have been doing it for centuries. This method of cooking imparts a unique flavour which, thanks to the vegetables' natural sugars and the small amount of added sugar, is enhanced by gentle caramelisation. To enjoy it at its best, this salad should be eaten warm - not hot or cold.

Method First, make the vinaigrette by putting all the ingredients into a bowl and whisking thoroughly - or put them into a stoppered bottle and shake vigorously.

To make the salad, preheat the oven to 180˚C/350˚F/gas mark 4. Put the onions in a baking dish and roast for about 1 hour, or until they feel soft. Peel off the outer skins and cut the white flesh into quarters.

Rinse the capers in running water, then squash them gently with your fingertips. Put the onions and cucumber into a serving dish, scatter over the capers and sprinkle with the Special vinaigrette.

Roast tomatoes with garlic

Serves 4

4 large tomatoes, halved

2 tablespoons fresh wholemeal
* breadcrumbs*

1 garlic clove, very finely chopped

6 large basil leaves, roughly torn

Tomatoes came to Europe from South America with the Spanish explorers, and the Sephardic Jews took them back to North America and to the Middle East when the Inquisition forced them out of Spain.

The sharp taste of garlic and the wonderful aroma of basil have made this a popular dish which can be served hot as a vegetable or cold as an appetiser or part of a buffet. Simple to make, it is a rich source of the protective antioxidant lycopene, in the tomatoes, and the cholesterol-lowering benefits of garlic.

Method Preheat the oven to 180°C/350°F/gas mark 4. Put the tomatoes into a shallow baking tray, cut side up.

Mix together the breadcrumbs, garlic and basil. Push the breadcrumb mix gently into the tomato halves. Bake for 20 minutes.

Braised carrots

Serves 4

3 tablespoons olive oil

8 young carrots, with the bottom
  1cm (1/2in) of their leaves

About 200ml (7fl oz) vegetable
  stock - see recipe for Barley
  with mushrooms and marjoram
  (page 47) or use a good-quality,
  low-salt cube or bouillon powder
  such as Kallo or Marigold

1 tablespoon finely chopped mint

4 tablespoons raisins

2 tablespoons finely chopped
  flat-leaf parsley

Carrots are widely used in all Jewish communities, from the coldest parts of eastern Europe to the kitchens of the Mediterranean and the hot-spots of the Middle East, Asia and India. Adding mint and raisins is typical of Middle Eastern and north African Jewish and Muslim cooking.

Method Heat the olive oil in a large frying pan and sauté the carrots gently until golden all over - about 6 minutes. Add enough stock (or water) just to cover. Tip in the mint and raisins. Cover and simmer until the carrots are almost tender - about 15 minutes.

Uncover and bring to a brisk boil until most of the liquid has evaporated. Scatter with the parsley to serve.

Health note Rich in cancer-fighting beta-carotene, carrots are of the few vegetables that are better cooked than eaten raw, as the cooking process makes the nutrients easier for your body to extract. The oil in this recipe improves absorption of beta-carotene, a fat-soluble nutrient that is also good for night vision.

Courgette salad

Serves 4

8 baby courgettes
Juice of 1/2 lemon
3 tablespoons extra-virgin olive oil
1/2 teaspoon ground allspice

Most squashes have little flavour but, like sponges, they soak up the tastes of herbs and spices – which is why they are paired here with allspice. Popular throughout the Ottoman Empire, allspice isn't, as many people think, a mixture of lots of spices; it's the whole or powdered seeds of a tropical tree called *Pimenta officinalis* with an intriguing flavour that tastes like a mixture of nutmeg, cloves and cinnamon. Sometimes referred to as Jamaica pepper, it's widely used in Turkey and north Africa.

Method Simmer the courgettes in salted water until soft. Drain and squeeze gently (use a sieve or muslin). Chop coarsely.

Mix together the lemon juice, oil and allspice. Pour over the courgettes and serve cold.

Health note There is no need to peel these baby vegetables, which means you get fibre and beta-carotene from this recipe as well as vitamin C from the lemon juice and digestive benefits from the allspice.

Celery braised in walnut oil

Serves 4

2 celery hearts, halved lengthways
  (save the leaves)
4 tablespoons walnut oil
3 tablespoons lemon juice
1 teaspoon brown caster sugar
1 teaspoon chopped sage

Celery has always been a popular vegetable. Widely used in stews and casseroles in western European and North American Ashkenazi cooking, it is also favoured by Sephardi cooks for its unique flavour. Here, simply braised over a low heat to preserve its nutrients, it has a surprisingly delicate and interesting taste.

Method Put all of the ingredients, including the celery leaves, together in a pan wide enough to hold the celery in a single layer.

Turn the celery hearts over gently so that they're covered with the liquid ingredients. Cover and simmer gently for about 35 minutes.

Health note 100g (3½oz) of celery contain only 7 calories, and you really do use more to chew and digest it than it provides. Although very poor in conventional nutrients, celery has great medicinal value as a gentle diuretic. Ensure you eat the leaves for their beta-carotene and folic acid.

Lettuce with anchovies

Serves 4

4 Little Gem lettuces, halved
  lengthways
1 tablespoon fennel seeds
150ml (1/4 pint) olive oil
About 300ml (1/2 pint) vegetable
  stock – see recipe for Barley with
  mushrooms and marjoram
  (page 47) or use a good-quality,
  low-salt cube or bouillon powder
  such as Kallo or Marigold
8 canned anchovy fillets, preferably
  in olive oil

The ancient Greek physicians knew that wild lettuce was a great cure for insomnia. They used to extract the sticky sap from the stalks and concentrate it to make a potent sleeping draught. All modern lettuces are descended from the same family and, although they're not so potent, they are still calming, relaxing and mildly soporific.

The ancient Romans loved to combine the harsh taste of salted anchovies with the slight bitterness of lettuce. Whether this preference was taken to Rome by the Jews or acquired from the Romans by the Jews who settled there isn't known. It's certain, however, that both ingredients appeal to Jewish palates, and you'll find variations on this recipe in the Jewish communities of Spain, Portugal, southern France, Greece and Italy.

Method Preheat the oven to 180°C/350°F/gas mark 4. Put the lettuce halves into a casserole dish. Scatter with the fennel seeds and pour over the oil.

Heat the stock and pour over the lettuces, ensuring that they're just covered; top up with boiling water if necessary. Cover with foil and bake for 25 minutes.

Remove from the oven, arrange the anchovy fillets over the lettuces and return to the oven, covered with foil, for 10 minutes.

Nutty spinach with raisins

Serves 4

50g (2oz) seedless raisins

25g (1oz) pinenuts

2 tablespoons olive oil

1 garlic clove, very finely sliced

1kg (2¼lb) baby spinach

Juice of ½ lemon

The combination of spinach, nuts and dried fruits is a common favourite with Jews and Muslims in the Middle East and north Africa. This recipe comes from Rome, but it was almost certainly taken there by Jewish traders during the days of the Roman Empire. It has now migrated into the general realm of Italian cooking and is normally eaten warm rather than hot.

Delicious served cold as a salad, but if you're having a non-meat meal, try crumbling feta cheese as well as (or instead of) the lemon juice on top.

Method Soak the raisins in freshly boiled water for 10 minutes and dry-roast the pinenuts.

Put the olive oil into a large pan and sauté the garlic very gently for 2 minutes. Wash the spinach, even if the packaging says it's ready-washed, and add to the garlic pan with only the water clinging to the leaves. Cook, covered, over a gentle heat until the spinach is wilted – not more than 5 minutes.

Drain the raisins and add to the spinach with the pinenuts, stirring them in gently. Serve with the lemon juice squeezed on top.

Health note With all the nutrients in spinach (especially the beta-carotene), protein and minerals from the pine nuts, and heart-protective properties from garlic, this is exceptionally healthy. Adding feta cheese provides a bonus of extra calcium.

Boulangère potatoes

Serves 4

About 2 tablespoons olive oil

3 medium onions, finely sliced

700g (1¹/₂lb) old potatoes, peeled
  and thinly sliced

2 bay leaves, torn in half

1 garlic clove, finely chopped

2 tablespoons thyme leaves

700ml (1¹/₄ pints) chicken stock –
  see recipe for Chicken soup with
  matzo dumplings (page 66), or
  use a good-quality, low-salt
  stock cube or bouillon
  powder such as Kallo or Marigold

Black pepper

Potatoes are one of the vegetable mainstays of Ashkenazi cooking from Eastern Europe, where they were one of the few abundant vegetables. This recipe also has the more Mediterranean influences of garlic, thyme and bay leaves.

I haven't been able to find the origins of the title, but this is a popular French/Jewish recipe and I can only guess that it was taken in its pot to the village *boulanger* (baker) – possibly before the start of Sabbath – hence the name *boulangère* (baker's wife). However it came to be named, it is extremely healthy.

Method Preheat the oven to 220°C/425°F/gas mark 7. Brush a little of the olive oil around a large casserole dish.

Gently sauté the onions in the remainder of the oil until soft but not brown. Put the onions in the base of the casserole. Arrange the potato slices in layers on top, with the bay leaves, garlic and thyme leaves distributed equally.

Pour over the stock and scatter over a few generous grindings of black pepper. Bake for 35 minutes, occasionally pushing the potatoes gently into the stock if necessary.

Aubergine rice

1 large aubergine, peeled and diced
About 2 teaspoons sea salt
3 tablespoons olive oil
1 medium onion, finely sliced
1 garlic clove, finely sliced
400g (14oz) long-grain white rice
1 litre (1³/4 pints) vegetable stock –
  see recipe for Barley with
  mushrooms and marjoram
  (page 47) or use a good-quality,
  low-salt stock cube or bouillon
  powder such as Kallo or Marigold

The wonderful aubergine has a truly ancient history; it has certainly been known in India for at least 3,000 years and was used in China several hundred years before the Common Era. Together with rice, it was introduced to Italy by the Arabs in the 10th century, but was already popular with Middle Eastern and Sephardic Jews.

This dish is a Sicilian version of risotto. As well as being a super-healthy side dish, it also makes a good starter or light meal – and you can serve it hot or cold.

Method Put the aubergines into a colander, sprinkle with salt, leave for 30 minutes, rinse thoroughly and wipe dry.

Warm the oil in a large, wide pan and sauté the onion and garlic until soft but not browned. Add the rice and stir until all the grains are covered with oil. Tip in the aubergine cubes and stir until covered with the oil. Start adding the stock, a ladleful at a time, and keep stirring until each ladleful is absorbed. Continue until you've used up all the stock and the rice is tender and nearly dry. Serve hot or cold. If serving it cold, you may have to stir in an extra tablespoon or so of olive oil.

Ceramic plate   This is a piece of Lambeth pottery, c. 1720. The script in the centre of the plate is the Hebrew word for meat and there is a similar plate for milk in the Museum of London. The Delft blue-and-white colouring is unusual on such a plate because the conventional colouring was red for meat and blue or green for dairy. It is probable that the plate was so labelled to help the servants keep the milk and meat utensils separate – this clearly belonged to an orthodox family.

main courses

Vegetarian cholent

Serves 4-6

2 tablespoons olive oil

1 onion, finely chopped

2 garlic cloves, finely chopped

225g (8oz) pot barley

*175g (6oz) canned butter beans
    (drained weight)*

*2 tablespoons chopped flat-leaf
    parsley*

*2 tablespoons flour, seasoned with
    4 grindings of black pepper*

*About 350g (12oz) old potatoes,
    unpeeled but thinly sliced*

*About 850ml (1½ pints) vegetable
    stock – see recipe for Barley with
    mushrooms and marjoram
    (page 47) or use a good-quality,
    low-salt stock cube or bouillon
    powder such as Kallo or Marigold*

For observant Jews throughout the world, it's forbidden to light a fire, turn on an oven or strike a match between the hours of sunset on Friday and sunset on Saturday. For this reason, the slow-cooked casserole is a common factor for Ashkenazi, Sephardi, Indian, Greek, Russian, Polish and British Jews. Whatever their culinary heritage, the principles remain the same. In the villages of eastern Europe, people took their own pot to the baker, where it went into the ovens when the last bread came out on Friday afternoon. At the end of the Sabbath, the pots were collected and taken home for the evening meal. The most common dish was *cholent*, and most housewives kept a pot that was used for nothing else. The British and American versions owe their origins to eastern Europe, where cholent was eaten to keep out the bitter cold of winter. Just the thought of this massive pot of fatty meat, beans, marrow bones, dumplings, potatoes and even chicken fat is enough to cause a heart attack – sorry, but this is the very worst of Jewish cooking.

According to Claudia Roden, in her wonderful *Book of Jewish Food,* cholent is an ancient descendant of the French cassoulet and gets its name from the medieval French *chaud* (hot) and *lent* (slow). The version here is much closer to that eaten by poor Jews who couldn't afford meat; *cholent* became lethal only with affluence. Serve with steamed broccoli florets mixed with crushed blanched almonds.

Method Preheat the oven to 180°C/350°F/gas mark 4. Heat the oil in a large flameproof casserole and gently sauté the onion and garlic until softened but not brown. Add the barley, beans and parsley.

Sprinkle the seasoned flour over the contents. Layer the potatoes on top and pour over the stock. Cover with a lid or aluminium foil and cook for 50 minutes.

Health note This recipe won't give you a heart attack and it will actually help to lower cholesterol, reduce blood pressure and protect your heart and circulatory system.

Lentil rissoles with crushed tomato sauce

Serves 4-6

For the rissoles

175g (6oz) lentils

About 4 tablespoons rapeseed or
  sunflower oil

1 medium onion, finely chopped

1 garlic clove, finely chopped

1 large carrot, grated

1 tablespoon finely chopped flat
  leaf parsley

1 teaspoon finely chopped fresh
  coriander leaves

1 teaspoon ground cumin

1 large egg, beaten

3 tablespoons fresh wholemeal
  breadcrumbs

6 tablespoons coarse matzo meal

For the crushed tomato sauce

5 medium tomatoes

Dash of Tabasco sauce

1 teaspoon demerara sugar

150ml (1/4 pint) olive oil

6 basil leaves

From southern Europe to the Middle East and India, lentils have been a staple food for centuries. Lentil rissoles may sound like a music-hall-joke vegetarian recipe, but properly handled they're versatile, extremely nutritious and they taste great too.

Serve with Warm onion salad with cucumbers and capers (see page 82) and fresh garden peas. These rissoles can also be served cold if you leave out the Crushed tomato sauce and serve them with a Pomegranate with avocado salad (see page 75) or even a tomato and spring onion salad with Special vinaigrette (see page 82).

Method First, make the rissoles. Wash the lentils thoroughly and simmer in boiling water according to the packet instructions – usually about 20-25 minutes, but some lentils need soaking, then cooking for up to 1 hour. Drain well.

While they're cooking, heat the oil and gently sauté the onion and garlic until soft but not brown. Add the carrot and continue cooking gently for 5 more minutes. Stir in the lentils, herbs and cumin and heat gently for another 5 minutes. Pour into a large heatproof bowl, add the egg and breadcrumbs and combine thoroughly until the mixture holds its shape, adding more breadcrumbs if necessary.

Using your hands, form into 4-6 rissoles. Put the matzo meal onto a dinner plate and dip each rissole into it, covering all over. Put about 4 tablespoons olive oil into a frying pan and fry the rissoles, in batches if necessary, for about 5 minutes each side, until golden, adding more oil as required.

Put all the ingredients for the sauce into a blender or food-processor and whizz until well combined. Warm through, and pour the sauce over the rissoles to serve.

Health note Lentils contains protein, B vitamins, iron, zinc and calcium. Combined with carrots and fresh herbs, for beta-carotene and good digestion, these rissoles have the added bonus of huge amounts of protective lycopene from the Crushed tomato sauce.

Mediterranean medley

Serves 4

2 garlic cloves, finely chopped

1 onion, finely chopped

4 tablespoons olive oil

1 teaspoon chopped oregano

4 tomatoes, finely sliced

250g (9oz) buffalo mozzarella,
sliced to the same size as the
tomatoes

8 courgettes, sliced to the same
size as the tomatoes and
mozzarella

4 tablespoons grated Parmesan
cheese

6 dill fronds

I was eleven years old when my father took us on holiday to France. After a week driving through the war-ravaged areas of the north of the country, we finally ended up in Nice, where for the first time I tasted the wonders of Mediterranean cooking.

One evening we ate with a Jewish family my father had known before the war. In 1950, it was almost impossible to get Kosher meat in that part of the world, so we ate this wonderful vegetarian dish. I'd never seen courgettes or mozzarella cheese and never tasted olive oil. Protein, calcium, vitamins and flavour abound in this simple dish – and it's just as good hot or cold. Serve with baby new potatoes boiled in their skins.

Method Preheat the oven to 180°C/350°F/gas mark 4. Sauté the garlic and onion gently in the olive oil until soft but not browned. Mix with the oregano and put them in the base of a large, shallow casserole dish. Arrange the tomatoes, mozzarella and courgettes alternately in layers on top. Cover with aluminium foil and bake for about an hour, or until the juices start running.

Scatter with the Parmesan, turn up the oven to 200°C/400°F/gas mark 6 and bake for a further 15 minutes. Serve with the dill fronds on top.

Spiced vegetable lasagne

Serves 6

For the white sauce
50g (2oz) unsalted butter
3 tablespoons flour
$^1/_2$ teaspoon ground cumin
500ml (18fl oz) soya milk

For the lasagne
1 large onion, finely chopped
1 garlic clove, finely chopped
About 3 tablespoons olive oil
3 courgettes, diced
1 large aubergine, diced
3 large, thin-skinned tomatoes,
  coarsely chopped
1 tablespoon tomato purée
3 tablespoons finely chopped fresh
  oregano (or 1 tablespoon dried)
400g (14oz) dried lasagne,
  blanched for 3 minutes in boiling
  water – or according to the
  packet instructions
3 tablespoons grated Parmesan
  cheese
6 dill fronds

Italy is one of the better countries for vegetarian travellers. Although there are few native vegetarians, so much of their wonderful Mediterranean culinary repertoire is based on non-meat dishes that there is inevitably a reasonable vegetarian choice in most cafés and restaurants. This Italian Jewish favourite became widely popular as a result of the massive increase in tourism during the 1960s and 70s.

Serve with a large bowl of mixed leaves and spring onion salad with Special vinaigrette (see page 82).

Method First, make the white sauce. Melt the butter gently in a large frying pan. Take off the heat and stir in the flour and cumin. Return to a gentle heat and cook, stirring continuously, for 2 minutes. Gradually add the soya milk, still stirring continuously, until thickened.

To make the lasagne, preheat the oven to 220°C/425°F/gas mark 7. Sweat the onion and garlic gently in 2 tablespoons of the oil until softened but not browned. Add the courgettes, aubergine, tomatoes, tomato purée and oregano and continue cooking for 5 minutes, stirring continuously.

Grease a wide, shallow, ovenproof pasta dish with the olive oil. Put in one layer of blanched lasagne sheets. Tip in half the vegetable mixture and a third of the white sauce. Add another layer of blanched lasagne sheets. Follow with the remainder of the vegetable mixture and another third of the sauce. Add another layer of blanched lasagne sheets and the remainder of the sauce, making sure the pasta is well covered with the sauce.

Bake for 15 minutes. Remove from the oven, scatter with the Parmesan and dill and return to the oven for 5 minutes.

Health note Healthy enough on its own, with all the protective benefits of onions, garlic and the vegetables, the white sauce is made here with soya milk for extra isoflavones. These hormone-like chemicals help protect against osteoporosis and menstrual problems.

Fish with prunes and tomatoes

Serves 4

4 cod steaks

*8 ready-to-eat stoned prunes,
  halved*

8 cherry tomatoes, halved

4 tablespoons olive oil

150ml (1/4 pint) dry white wine

4 large dill fronds

Black pepper

The combination of dried fruits with meat, poultry and fish was popular from the earliest times throughout the Middle East, north Africa and the Mediterranean, including Greece. In this incredibly healthy recipe from Thessalonika, the only fat comes from the heart-protective monounsaturated fat in the olive oil.

Delicious served with noodles or fried rice and Celery braised in walnut oil (see page 86).

Method Preheat the oven to 180°C/350°F/gas mark 4. Put the fish in one layer in a large casserole or baking tin. Arrange the prunes and tomatoes around the fish. Pour over the olive oil and white wine, then add the dill fronds and 3 grindings of black pepper.

Cover with a lid or aluminium foil and bake for 30 minutes.

Health note The fish provides protein, vitamins and minerals, especially iodine, which is essential for proper functioning of the thyroid gland and is frequently deficient in the average diet. Tomatoes offer the carotenoid lycopene, which protects against breast and prostate cancers. And prunes are nature's miracle fruit – weight for weight, they supply the highest score of ORAC units (see page 13) of all foods. Just 100g (3 1/2oz) will give you well over the optimum 5,000 protective units a day to prevent ageing, degenerative disease, heart and circulatory problems and, believe it or not, wrinkles.

Coconut fish

Serves 4

1 onion, finely chopped

1/2 fennel bulb, finely chopped

2 tablespoons olive oil

250ml (9fl oz) coconut milk

2 heaped tablespoons live natural yogurt

1/2 teaspoon grated nutmeg

1 teaspoon ground cumin

1 saffron strand

250ml (9fl oz) fish stock – see recipe for Fish with watercress (page 59) or use a good-quality, low-salt stock cube or bouillon powder such as Kallo or Marigold

4 large tilapia (or red snapper) fillets or 8 smaller ones

4 tablespoons chopped parsley

Coconut milk is a popular ingredient with the Jews of India, but this is a Sephardic recipe from Cuba. It is traditionally made with tilapia, a fish that comes from the Sea of Galilee. Christians believe the two large black marks on either side of the fish were left by the thumb and forefinger of St Peter, hence its other name, St Peter's fish. It's also popular in the cuisine of Arab countries, where it is known as *mousht*. And tilapia is the most widely used fish in Israel.

Serve with plain boiled rice and a tomato and spring onion salad with Special vinaigrette (see page 82).

Method Gently sauté the onion and fennel in the oil until softened but not brown. Mix in the coconut milk, yogurt, nutmeg, cumin, saffron and stock. Add the fish fillets, covering them with the coconut mixture.

Cover and simmer until the fish is cooked – about 10 minutes. Serve scattered with the parsley.

Health note This wonderfully healthy dish is virtually free from harmful saturated fat, full of protein, calcium and other minerals and it tastes fabulous.

Herring in oatmeal

Serves 4

50g (2oz) coarse oatmeal

4 grindings of black pepper

4 large herring, gutted and split (ask your fishmonger), washed and patted dry

50g (2oz) unsalted butter

2 lemons, halved

Opposite: *Coconut fish*

Herring in all forms has been a staple food for Jews in eastern and northern Europe and in the UK. This recipe, from a Jewish family in Glasgow, is the ideal fusion of two cultures; the Scots also have herring as a staple part of their diet and they have the great tradition of using oats, one of the healthiest of all cereals.

Serve with cold Broad beans with beetroot and Magic mayonnaise with additions of your choice (see page 81) or warm baby potatoes boiled in their jackets with Special vinaigrette (see page 82).

Method Mix together the oatmeal and pepper.

Lay the herring skin side down in a grill pan and sprinkle generously with the oatmeal mixture. Dot with butter and grill under a moderate heat for about 12 minutes. Put the lemon halves on the side of each plate to serve.

Health note No matter how you serve it, herring is the richest source of essential fatty acids which are so important for brain development and function as well as being naturally anti-inflammatory and helping relieve the problems of dyslexia, ADHD and general learning difficulties in children. It also provides large amounts of the essential vitamin D, without which the body can't absorb calcium to build and maintain strong bones.

Hot and sour fish stew

Serves 4-6

25g (1oz) tamarind pulp (available from speciality Indian food shops)

2 tablespoons olive oil

1 white onion, finely chopped

2 tablespoons mild chilli paste

Juice of 1 lime

450g (1lb) fresh salmon, pulled into bite-sized pieces along the grain of the flesh

Whether they come from eastern Europe, Persia, Palestine or Israel, both Ashkenazi and Sephardi Jews have always enjoyed the combination of sweet and sour tastes. This recipe uses tamarind, traditionally thought of as an Indian ingredient, but equally at home in Jewish recipes in Iraq and Syria. Historically, tamarind pods have been used as much in Indian and Arabic medicine as they have in food. Preparing tamarind pulp from the commercially available dried blocks may seem like a lot of bother, but it's really worth the effort for its unique flavour.

Serve with Green beans with onion and thyme (see page 78) or a mixed-leaf salad with Special vinaigrette (see page 82).

Method Put the tamarind pulp into a small bowl. Pour on 125g (4fl oz) boiling water. Soak for about 20 minutes and push the pulp through a sieve with a small wooden spoon.

Heat the oil in a large saucepan and gently sauté the onion until softened but not brown. Add the chilli paste and cook gently, stirring continuously, for 5 minutes. Pour in the liquid from the tamarind pulp. Add the lime juice and bring to a simmer. Add the fish and stir until covered with the sauce. Cover and simmer gently until the fish is cooked - about 4-5 minutes.

Health note Heart-protective essential fatty acids from the salmon and the circulatory stimulus from the chilli make this as healthy as it is tasty.

Trout in papaya sauce

Serves 4

8 fresh trout fillets

Juice of 1 lemon

1 tablespoon Tabasco sauce

4 tablespoons flour, seasoned with
  black pepper

200ml (7fl oz) olive oil

2 papayas

25g (1oz) unsalted butter

1 standard glass dry white wine

Because of the demands of the Jewish dietary laws, Jews have developed interesting ways of preparing fish. Many less orthodox Jews are happy to eat in non-Kosher restaurants or homes of non-Jewish friends, and although they wouldn't consume meat, fish would be acceptable.

A non-orthodox broadcasting colleague of mine is a keen fisherman whose freezer is always full of delicious trout. He's also an inventive cook and served this wonderful dish one very wet Sunday lunchtime. It is delicious with Aubergine rice (see page 91) or Pomegranate with avocado salad (page 75).

Method Put the fish in a large shallow dish.

Mix together the lemon juice and Tabasco sauce, pour over the fish and leave, covered, to marinate for at least 30 minutes. Take the fish out of the marinade and dust with the seasoned flour. Fry in the oil for about 3 minutes each side. Put onto a large plate and keep warm.

Mash the papaya flesh. Melt the butter gently in a clean pan. Add the wine and papaya flesh and warm gently, stirring continuously. Serve the fish with the papaya sauce on top.

Health note The heart and brain benefits of oily fish, the circulatory boost from the chilli in the Tabasco sauce, and the enzymes and carotenoids from the papaya make this dish an excellent boost to your health as well as a delight to eat.

Spinach fish cakes with gooseberry sauce

Serves 4

350g (12oz) baby spinach leaves

225g (8oz) mashed potatoes

350g (12oz) canned salmon
  (drained weight)

2 eggs

6 tablespoons medium matzo meal

About 150ml (1/4 pint) rapeseed or
  sunflower oil for shallow frying

350g (12oz) gooseberries

2 tablespoons finely chopped mint

1 tablespoon runny honey

When I first left home to study in London, I shared a very primitive two-room flat with four friends. None of them had the faintest inkling of how to boil an egg, and we were all extremely hard-up. We put 10s (that's 50p) a week into a kitty and, as I was the only one who could cook - allegedly - I had the job of feeding all five of us.

The best practical cook in my family was my Auntie Leah, my mother's unmarried sister, who was the peripatetic carer for the entire family. I used to phone her in desperation for ideas for nourishing meals, and this was her recipe for a cheap and cheerful alternative to the traditional fried *gefilte* fish. Everyone loved them and I still make them to this day. The sauce was a much later addition from my wife Sally when we had a glut of gooseberries in the garden.

Serve with cucumber salad made with peeled, thinly sliced cucumber drizzled with Special vinaigrette (see page 82) and sprinkled with finely chopped flat-leaf parsley.

Method Wash the spinach (even if it's 'ready-washed'). Put into a large pan with just the water clinging to its leaves. Cover and heat, shaking occasionally, until just wilted. Chop roughly. Transfer to a large bowl with the potatoes and drained salmon and mix well.

Beat the eggs in a shallow bowl. Tip the matzo meal into another shallow bowl. Using your hands, mould the fish mixture into 8 burger shapes. Dip them first into the eggs, then into the matzo meal. Shallow fry, in batches, for 3 minutes each side. Keep warm.

Put the gooseberries into another pan with the mint. Add about 150ml (1/4 pint) water and the honey and simmer until the fruit becomes a pulp - about 10 minutes. Strain, pushing the fruit through a sieve with a wooden spoon. Return to the pan and reheat gently.

Serve the fish cakes with the sauce on the side.

Health note There are wonderful nutrients in the spinach, energy from the mashed potatoes, essential fatty acids from the salmon and fabulous fresh flavours in mint and gooseberries.

Chicken in orange sauce

Serves 6

*6 plump chicken thighs, skin
  removed*

*Juice and finely chopped peel of
  2 large oranges*

2 teaspoons ground turmeric

1 teaspoon black pepper

3 tablespoons olive oil

1 onion, finely chopped

2 garlic cloves, finely chopped

*200ml (7fl oz) chicken stock – see
  recipe for Chicken soup with
  matzo dumplings (page 66) or
  use a good-quality, low-salt
  stock cube or bouillon powder
  such as Kallo or Marigold*

150g (5oz) mushrooms, sliced

3 large sprigs of tarragon

You'd be forgiven for thinking that any form of poultry with orange sauce was part of the French *haute cuisine* tradition, but you'd be wrong. Jews have been cultivating citrus fruits since biblical times, as one of them, the citron (which looks like a very large lemon), is an essential part of the religious festival of Sukkot, the Feast of Tabernacles. Similar to the Christian harvest festival, it celebrates the produce of vineyards, fields and orchards.

Although the citron has a wonderful aroma, it's not normally eaten raw, but the Jews became experts at growing other citrus fruits, which they took to ancient Rome, Spain and the rest of the Mediterranean.

Serve with Spiced leeks (see page 71) or potatoes mashed with olive oil and chopped flat-leaf parsley.

Method Put the chicken pieces, orange juice and peel, turmeric and pepper into a large bowl. Stir well to coat the chicken and leave covered in the fridge for at least 2 hours or overnight.

Heat the oil in a large flameproof casserole and gently sauté the onion and garlic until just starting to soften. Take the chicken pieces out of the marinade, add to the casserole and brown all over, turning frequently. Tip in the marinade and stock and bring to a simmer. Add the mushrooms and tarragon. Simmer, covered, for about 45 minutes or until the chicken is tender.

Health note Oranges are widely used in Jewish cooking, and this low-fat recipe has the benefits of protein, vitamins and essential oils from the orange skin as well as the cancer-fighting properties of turmeric.

Chicken with mango glaze

Serves 4
200ml (7fl oz) mango juice
4 plump spring onions
1 tablespoon Dijon mustard
Leaves of 1 large sprig of rosemary
1 mango
4 chicken breasts

The history of Jews in Cuba is fascinating. The gradual demise of the Ottoman Empire, which was still in evidence until the First World War, and equal persecution of Jews and Muslims by Christians resulted in emigration from Turkey, the Balkans, Syria and other parts of the Middle East. Some of these displaced people travelled to Cuba, where, whether they were Jews or Arabs, the Cubans lumped them all together as *turkos*. These turko-Sephardic Jews were at home with the Spanish language and customs, but in the 1920s there was an influx of eastern European Jews whom the locals dubbed *polacos*. They ended up in Cuba because the USA placed strict quotas on immigrants fleeing the pogroms of Russia and Poland.

The small surviving community makes good use of local produce in their Kosher cooking, and this recipe, which comes from Cuba, tastes great as well as containing huge amounts of protective antioxidants and essential nutrients. Serve with Turnips and carrots with garlic (see page 74) and wild rice.

Method Preheat the oven to 180°C/350°F/gas mark 4. Put the mango juice, spring onions, mustard, rosemary and the flesh of the mango into a blender or food-processor and whizz until smooth.

Put the chicken breasts into a large, shallow, ovenproof dish and drizzle with the mango mixture. Roast for about 40 minutes, basting frequently, until the chicken is thoroughly cooked.

Serve with the sauce poured over the chicken.

Poussins stuffed with chicken livers and veal

Serves 4

4 poussins

Olive oil

Salt and black pepper

1 onion, finely chopped

½ garlic clove, finely chopped

*225g (8oz) mixed veal and chicken
    livers, minced*

*2 heaped tablespoons fresh
    breadcrumbs*

1 teaspoon tomato purée

*1 tablespoon finely chopped
    flat-leaf parsley*

*About 150ml (¼ pint) chicken
    stock – see recipe for Chicken
    soup with matzo dumplings
    (page 66) or use a good-quality,
    low-salt stock cube or bouillon
    powder such as Kallo or Marigold*

I enjoyed a version of this recipe with Jewish friends who owned an ancient but working olive mill in the south of France. The chickens were free-range, and the French, because they've never subscribed to the intensive rearing of calves, are far less squeamish about eating veal.

Delicious with Sweet and sour courgettes (see page 71) and baby potatoes boiled in their jackets.

Method Preheat the oven to 200°C/400°F/gas mark 6. Drizzle the poussins with olive oil and sprinkle them with black pepper and a little salt. Roast for 20 minutes. While they're cooking, heat 2 tablespoons olive oil in a largish frying pan and gently soften the onion and garlic for 2 minutes. Add the veal and chicken livers and cook thoroughly for about 5 minutes. Add the breadcrumbs, tomato purée, parsley and some of the stock, and continue cooking, stirring continuously, for 3 minutes, adding more stock as necessary to get the consistency of a stuffing.

Use this mixture to stuff the cavities of the birds. Put them back into the oven, reduce the heat to 180°C/350°F/gas mark 4 and roast for another 30 minutes.

Health note Rich in protein, iron and B vitamins and very low in fat, this mixture of chicken, veal and liver is a marriage made in the culinary heaven of France.

Chicken and chickpea curry

Serves 4

4 tablespoons sesame oil

1 onion, finely chopped

3 garlic cloves, finely chopped

1 green chilli, deseeded and finely chopped

1 level tablespoon curry powder

4 skinless chicken breasts, cut into strips along the grain of the meat

2.5cm (1in) ginger root, peeled and grated

2 dessertspoons tamarind paste

600ml (1 pint) chicken stock – see recipe for Chicken soup with matzo dumplings (page 66) or use a good-quality, low-salt stock cube or bouillon powder such as Kallo or Marigold

200g (7oz) canned chickpeas (drained weight), drained and rinsed

4 tablespoons coriander leaves, roughly torn

It's possible that there were Jews in India by the end of the twelfth century. There was an influx of Sephardi Jews, as you would expect, from Spain and Portugal, but also from Holland, where there was a large community, during the thirteenth to sixteenth centuries. The Dutch were probably the most important spice traders in Europe, and it was India, this vast continent of spices, that presented great business opportunities to the Jews, who traded with the Dutch East India Company. During the 1980s, I worked in a clinic in one of the original canal-side spice warehouses, and you could still smell the lingering and evocative perfume of pepper, nutmeg and cloves. One of the main areas in which all the Jews settled was Cochin, a south-west coastal city and province, where they soon fused the local spices and cooking styles with their Kosher traditions.

Although tamarind would have been a new taste for the Europeans, for those Jews who came much later from the Middle East, it was already a favourite spice. It adds an intriguing sweetness to this sharp curry and provides the added benefit of being a wonderful digestive aid.

Serve with Courgette salad (page 86) and plain boiled rice.

Method Put the oil into a large pan or flameproof casserole. Gently sauté the onion, garlic and chilli until softened but not brown – about 5 minutes. Add the curry powder, mix thoroughly and continue cooking for 2 minutes. Tip in the chicken, ginger and tamarind paste and cook, stirring continuously, until the chicken is golden all over. Add the stock and simmer until the chicken is tender – about 35 minutes.

Stir in the chickpeas and coriander and continue simmering until the chickpeas are heated through – about 7 minutes.

Roast duck with cherries

Serves 4

1.8kg (about 4lb) oven-ready
*   duckling*
2 tablespoons olive oil
1 medium onion, finely sliced
1 heaped tablespoon flour
250ml (9fl oz) chicken stock – see
*   recipe for Chicken soup with*
*   matzo dumplings (page 66) or*
*   use a good-quality, low-salt stock*
*   cube or bouillon powder such as*
*   Kallo or Marigold*
50ml (2fl oz) port or Kosher
*   dessert wine*
1 tablespoon runny honey
450g (1lb) cherries, pitted
1 teaspoon ground cinnamon
1 star anise
Juice of 1 lemon

Duck and goose have always been part of Ashkenazi cooking throughout eastern Europe and Germany, but duck was also a favourite in the Middle East and Asia. Some great recipes travelled with Jewish families who left Persia for Britain and America. This dish came from one of my aunt's Polish in-laws and is a firm favourite. Serve with Boulangère potatoes (see page 90) and Braised carrots (see page 85).

Method Preheat the oven to 220°C/425°F/gas mark 7. Prick the duck all over with a fork. Cover loosely with foil and put on a trivet in a roasting tin containing at least 2.5cm (1in) boiling water. Roast for 15 minutes.

Remove from the oven and pour away the water and all the fat that has dropped into it. Take the duck off the trivet, return it to the roasting tin and put back into the oven. Reduce the heat to 180°C/350°F/gas mark 4 and continue roasting until the total cooking time is 20 minutes per 450g (1lb).

Heat the oil in a saucepan and gently sauté the onion for 2 minutes. Mix in the flour, stirring well, and continue cooking over a gentle heat for 2 more minutes. Add the stock, port or Kosher dessert wine, honey, cherries, cinnamon and star anise. Simmer until starting to thicken, stirring occasionally. Pour in the lemon juice and keep warm until the duck is cooked, carved and ready to serve. Remove the star anise from the sauce and serve poured over the duck.

Health note Although duck is perceived as being fatty, this cooking method removes most of the fat. As long as you don't eat the skin (delicious though it is), the end result is a low-fat dish full of iron, protein and B vitamins. The cherries add wonderful flavour and an abundance of antioxidant phytochemicals.

Pigeons with juniper berries

Serves 4

About 6 tablespoons olive oil

12 button onions

*3 slices of smoked beef, cut into
  strips*

4 small pigeons

1 tablespoon flour

*500ml (18fl oz) chicken stock – see
  recipe for Chicken soup with
  matzo dumplings (page 66) or
  use a good-quality, low-salt stock
  cube or bouillon powder such as
  Kallo or Marigold*

8 juniper berries, lightly crushed

3 large sprigs of parsley

2 sprigs of sage

*2 bay leaves, broken in half down
  the spine*

*1 celery stick, with leaves, roughly
  chopped*

Although goose was popular among the Ashkenazi Jews of Poland and pigeon and quail were widely eaten in the Mediterranean, North Africa and Egypt as part of the Sephardic tradition, these birds never seemed very popular with British Jewry. Certainly neither my mother, her sisters nor any others in our vast extended family ever served them. Because of the requirements of ritual slaughter, game birds that had been shot weren't Kosher – although quail and pigeon were traditionally caught or specially bred. Even duck was a rarity in Ashkenazi homes, although it was much more popular in the Sephardic culture.

You can substitute quail for the pigeons, but serve 2 per person – and the only way to eat these small birds is with your fingers. Serve with Red cabbage with apples and caraway (see page 70), Broad beans in olive oil (see page 73) and potatoes mashed with olive oil.

Method Heat the oil in a large flameproof casserole and sauté the onions until just coloured – about 3 minutes. Add the smoked beef and continue cooking for a further 3 minutes until the beef begins to turn brown. Remove the onions and beef from the pan. Adding more oil if necessary, brown the pigeons all over – 2 at a time if your casserole isn't large enough to move them around easily. Take out of the pan.

Sprinkle the flour into the remaining oil, mix thoroughly until well combined and gradually add the chicken stock, stirring continuously until thickened. Pour into a heatproof jug.

Put the onions and smoked beef back into the casserole. Add half the stock, along with the juniper berries, parsley, sage, bay leaves and celery.

Arrange the pigeons on top and pour over the remainder of the stock. Cover tightly and simmer gently for about 50 minutes, until the pigeons are tender, adding extra stock or boiling water if the dish seems to be drying out. Put 1 pigeon on each plate and strain the sauce over the birds.

Health note This typically French recipe for pigeon casserole is extremely low in saturated fat – the type that clogs your arteries. The combination of pigeon and beef supplies substantial quantities of iron. As well as adding typical Mediterranean flavours, the juniper berries are a rich source of protective antioxidants. The onions are heart-protective and help reduce blood cholesterol. Sage improves digestion and bay leaves are a gentle mood-enhancer.

Beef loaf with tomato sauce

Serves 4

700g (1^1/$_2$lb) good-quality braising
  beef (such as chuck steak, all
  visible fat removed, minced
225g (8oz) coarse matzo meal
1 onion, very finely chopped
2 eggs, beaten
1 tablespoon grated orange zest
1 tablespoon finely chopped mint
1 tablespoon flat-leaf parsley,
  finely chopped
^{1}/$_2$ teaspoon each ground
  cinnamon and ground cloves
2 dashes of Tabasco sauce
Rapeseed or sunflower oil, for
  greasing
200ml (7fl oz) stock – see recipe
  for Spiced lamb soup (page 64),
  but substitute beef for lamb, or
  use a good-quality, low-salt stock
  cube or bouillon powder such as
  Kallo or Marigold
1 quantity Crushed tomato sauce
  (see page 95)

There's nothing particularly Jewish about meat loaf, but it is a very popular Jewish dish, particularly in Ashkenazi communities. Known throughout the Yiddish-speaking peoples as *klops*, it was a factor of economy and convenience. The cheapest cuts of beef could be used for mince, and *klops* was a very practical dish as it could be eaten cold the following day with salad and a baked potato.

Although my mother's family all came from eastern Europe, she made this Dutch *klops* for my father; the recipe comes from my grandmother who lived in Amsterdam. It's made here with very lean beef to reduce the fat content, and the mint makes it easily digestible while the cinnamon and cloves add the exotic flavour of the Dutch East Indies that permeates a lot of Dutch Jewish cooking.

This recipe goes well with Roast tomatoes with garlic (see page 83) and baby new potatoes boiled in their jackets.

Method Preheat the oven to 180°C/350°F/gas mark 4.

In a large bowl, mix together the beef, matzo meal, onion, eggs, orange zest, mint, parsley, ground cinnamon and cloves and Tabasco sauce.

Heat the stock and keep it simmering.

Grease a 1-litre (1^3/4-pint) loaf tin (about 22 x 12 x 7cm or 9 x 5 x 2^3/4in) with a little oil – even if it's 'non-stick'. Put the meat mixture into the tin, packing it down firmly. Put the tin into a roasting tin half-filled with boiling water and bake for 40 minutes, pouring in the hot stock as the loaf dries out.

Turn out onto a serving platter. Pour over the Crushed tomato sauce to serve.

North African beef stew

Serves 6

1 calf's foot (optional)

3 tablespoons groundnut oil

2 onions, finely sliced

2 garlic cloves, finely sliced

1kg (2¹/₄lb) lean stewing beef, cubed

12 new potatoes, unpeeled

2 large carrots, cubed

6 eggs, in their shells

*350g (12oz) canned flageolet beans
   (drained weight)*

2 teaspoons ground allspice

*850ml (1¹/₂ pints) meat stock – see
   recipe for Spiced lamb soup
   (page 64) or use a good-quality,
   low-salt stock cube or bouillon
   powder such as Kallo or Marigold*

With the dominance of pre-packed supermarket food, people in northern Europe and the USA have grown increasingly separated from the reality of food. Children think milk comes from cartons, not cows, and fish fingers from the freezer, not the sea. It's hardly surprising, then, that we've become squeamish about what we eat. Offal, chicken's feet, calves' feet and other 'strange' bits and pieces are rarely used – which is sad as they're nutritious and usually inexpensive. Serve with Orange and olive salad (see page 77) and rice.

Method Preheat the oven to 180˚C/350˚F/gas mark 4. Put the calf's foot, if using, into boiling water for 2 minutes, then drain.

Heat the oil in a large flameproof casserole and gently sauté the onions and garlic until softened but not brown – about 5 minutes. Add the calf's foot and the rest of the ingredients, including the eggs in their shells, and bring to the boil. Put into the oven for 2 hours, adding more stock if it dries out.

Serve with 1 hard-boiled egg on each plate. When shelled, the egg will be a rich brown colour.

Health note Almost every cookbook written before the 1960s would have had a section on sick-room cooking – and that would have included calf's foot jelly, which is full of B vitamins, enzymes and protein. Although optional in this recipe, do have a go. You'll be amazed by the delicate flavour and wonderful full-bodied texture it gives to this traditional Moroccan variation of *cholent*.

Lamb on couscous

Serves 6

*700g (1¹/₂lb) stewing lamb, cubed
   and all visible fat removed*

*1.2 litres (2 pints) lamb stock – see
   Spiced lamb soup (page 64) or
   use a good-quality, low-salt stock
   cube or bouillon powder*

2 carrots, diced

2 onions, finely sliced

2 courgettes, cut into large cubes

1 turnip, cubed

3 cloves

3 bay leaves, broken in half

¹/₂ teaspoon sea salt

4 grindings of black pepper

2 tablespoons raisins

450g (1lb) couscous

This combination of a savoury meat dish with cloves is unmistakably Moroccan. If you imagine that the only place for cloves is in apple pie or in an orange to make mulled wine, you'll be missing out on one of the most distinctive flavours of this part of the world – served here with north African couscous. As long as you've trimmed the fat off the meat and skimmed the broth, this is a low-fat, high-protein meal which represents extremely good nutritional value for money, with no compromise in taste. Good with Braised carrots (page 85).

Method Put the lamb into a large saucepan. Pour in the stock, bring to the boil and simmer, covered, until the lamb is tender – about 1 hour. Skim off any fat. Add the carrots, onions, courgettes, turnip, cloves, bay leaves, salt, pepper and raisins. Simmer until the vegetables are cooked – about 10 minutes. Skim off any additional fat and keep warm.

Cook the couscous according to packet instructions, using the stock from the lamb instead of boiled water. Pile the couscous onto a large platter, with the lamb and vegetables arranged on top.

Health note Full of minerals and antioxidants from the root vegetables and extra fibre and iron from the raisins, this is an ideal recipe for building stamina, strength and natural immunity.

Lamb and lentils

Serves 4–6

4 lamb shanks (or 8 thick lamb
chops)

4 tablespoons olive oil

2 onions, finely sliced

1 large leek, thickly sliced
diagonally

3 garlic cloves, finely sliced

3 large carrots, cut into large cubes

1.2 litres (2 pints) lamb stock – see
recipe for Spiced lamb soup
(page 64) or use a good-quality,
low-salt stock cube or bouillon
powder such as Kallo or Marigold

250g (9oz) green or brown lentils

3 bay leaves

2 large sprigs of thyme

1 sprig of rosemary

The night before the Jews escaped in the great exodus from Egypt, their final meal was the Paschal lamb. Centuries later, Jews in every corner of the world remember this meal by the ritual of the roasted lamb shank (more likely to be a roasted chicken neck in modern homes), which is one of the symbolic foods displayed on the festive table of the Passover meal. Roasted lamb shank became a popular Jewish dish throughout the Middle East, and especially in Greece. Lentils were one of the earliest foods cultivated in 'the promised land'.

Serve with Beans in garlic (see page 78) and plain boiled rice.

Method Brown the lamb shanks (or chops) all over in the oil. Remove and set aside. Add the onions, leek and garlic and gently sauté until just softened. Add the carrots and continue to sauté for 5 minutes, stirring continuously.

Put the lamb and all the vegetables into a large flameproof casserole. Add the stock, lentils, bay leaves, thyme and rosemary. Bring to the boil, then simmer for about 1$^{1}/_{2}$ hours until everything is tender.

Remove the lamb, use a slotted spoon to pile the vegetables onto a large platter and put the lamb on top. Pour the remainder of the stock into a gravy bowl to serve.

Health note The lentils bring fibre, minerals and B vitamins to the low-fat protein of this succulent dish.

Lamb and lemon kebabs with hot red salsa

Serves 6

700g (1½lb) very lean minced lamb

Juice and grated zest of 1 large lemon

1 large egg (or 2 small ones), beaten

100g (3½oz) fine matzo meal

1 teaspoon ground cumin

5 tablespoons finely chopped mint

5 tablespoons frozen sweetcorn, completely defrosted and crushed

1 red pepper, deseeded and finely chopped

1 small red chilli, deseeded and finely chopped

2 tomatoes, finely chopped

2 shallots, finely chopped

Whether you cook this under the grill, in a griddle pan or, best of all, on a barbecue, you'll enjoy the traditional taste of these Jewish/Egyptian lamb kebabs with the fiery heat of chillies: a taste that has spread from the North African Jews of Tunisia to communities in Yemen, India, South America and finally back to Israel.

This dish goes well with Nutty spinach with raisins (see page 88) and parboiled potato wedges brushed with olive oil and baked for about 20 minutes at 200ºC/400ºF/gas mark 6.

Method Mix together the lamb, lemon juice and zest, egg(s), matzo meal, cumin and half the mint. Roll into 18 small sausage shapes, thread onto kebab sticks and leave in the fridge for 30 minutes. Put under a hot grill, or on a griddle or barbecue, for about 10 minutes, according to size, until well cooked.

While they're cooking, mix together the sweetcorn, red pepper, chilli, tomatoes and shallots. Serve the kebabs with the hot red salsa as a dip.

Health note This dish is full of health-promoting herbs and spices and is good for digestion, circulation and blood pressure. It's the ultimate healthy alternative to the doner kebab.

Spiced lamb cutlets

Serves 4

8 lamb cutlets

4 onions, quartered

175g (6oz) brown caster sugar

150ml (¼ pint) light soy sauce

1 teaspoon ground cinnamon

1 teaspoon ground cloves

4 generous grindings of black
  pepper

1cm (½in) ginger root, peeled and
  grated

Adding these spices to a meat dish is typically north African and also popular in parts of the Middle East. This recipe clearly illustrates the difference between the Jewish cooking of middle and eastern Europe and the Moorish influences on Jews who travelled in the opposite direction. In parts of the Middle East, this dish would be made with kid.

Serve with Roast tomatoes with garlic (see page 83) and baby new potatoes boiled in their jackets.

Method Preheat the oven to 180°C/350°F/gas mark 4. Put the cutlets into a large pan with the onions and just cover with water. Simmer gently for 10 minutes.

Meanwhile, heat the remainder of the ingredients gently in another saucepan.

Remove the cutlets and onions from their cooking liquid, add to the soy sauce mixture, coating thoroughly, and cook over a very low heat for 10 minutes. Transfer the cutlets, without the soy sauce mixture, to an ovenproof dish and roast until crisp - about 30 minutes.

Health note It's low in fat, with lots of protein and all the medicinal benefits of the spices.

Veal schnitzel

Serves 4

2 medium eggs

1 teaspoon Worcestershire sauce

6 tablespoons fine matzo meal

1 teaspoon mustard powder

3-4 grindings of black pepper

4 veal escalopes, beaten thin
  between 2 sheets of clingfilm
  with a meat mallet or rolling pin

4 tablespoons olive oil

1 lemon, quartered, to garnish

During the 1920s and early 30s, German and Austrian Jews probably had the most influence on the whole of European Jewry. In fact, they considered themselves to be a cut above the rest, especially those of eastern Europe. Many of their dishes were adopted and adapted by other communities, and the Wiener schnitzel, just like strudel and the other wonderful pastries of the coffee houses, spread from Vienna to Jews in Britain, France, Italy, Hungary and across the Atlantic to America.

In recent years, there has been a resistance to eating veal because of the terrible conditions calves are often reared in. Try to find a Kosher butcher who sells organic meat, the rearing of which forbids the use of crates, tethering and other cruel practices. Serve with Lettuce with anchovies (see page 87).

Method Beat the eggs with the Worcestershire sauce. Mix together the matzo meal, mustard powder and black pepper. Dip the escalopes in the egg mixture, then into the matzo meal. Fry in the oil until golden - about 2 minutes on each side. Garnish with the lemon quarters to serve.

Health note Veal has a very low fat content, as well as plenty of protein and B vitamins.

Calf's liver risotto

Serves 4

1 litre (1³/4 pints) chicken stock -
  see recipe for Chicken soup with
  matzo dumplings (page 66) or
  use a good-quality, low-salt stock
  cube or bouillon powder such as
  Kallo or Marigold
5 tablespoons olive oil
6 large spring onions, cut into large
  chunks diagonally
275g (10oz) arborio or carnaroli rice
Black pepper
450g (1lb) calf's liver, cut into strips
About 12 sage leaves, roughly
  torn

This recipe originates from the Jews of north-east Italy and combines the two Italian culinary traditions of risotto and cooking liver with sage. It was the Arabs who first took rice to Italy, where it still grows abundantly on the marshy plains of the River Po.

All offal has traditionally been used widely in Jewish communities, but for most British and American Jews, liver, tongue and possible kidneys are the only items that remain in common use. For the strictly orthodox, liver presents particular problems as it can't be rendered Kosher by the traditional method of soaking and salting. To ensure that every last trace of blood is removed, the liver needs to be cooked over an open fire or under a very hot grill within 72 hours of slaughtering and must not be allowed to sit in its own juices during cooking. The liver must be turned regularly and left exposed to the heat until it has cooked halfway through. Any liver that's going to be fried, baked or cooked in any other way must go through this process first.

This recipe is lovely with Broad beans in olive oil (see page 73) or an avocado and Cos lettuce salad with Special vinaigrette (see page 82)

Method Pour the stock into a saucepan and bring to a gentle simmer.

Put 2 tablespoons of the oil into a large frying pan or wok and gently sauté the spring onions until just soft – about 3 minutes. Tip in the rice and stir until all the grains are covered with oil. Ladle in about a quarter of the stock and stir vigorously until absorbed. Add the remainder of the stock, a ladleful at a time, still stirring until it has all been absorbed and the rice is just *al dente*. If necessary, add more stock or boiling water. Cover and keep warm.

Season the calf's liver with freshly ground black pepper and pan-fry quickly in the rest of the oil; it should take only about 1 minute, depending on the size of the strips and your individual taste. Stir the liver gently into the rice, tip into a large bowl and serve with the sage scattered on top.

Passover cup Although this cup would have been used for only one week of the year, it was clearly important enough for the owner to want one to accommodate his moustache. Moustache cups were very popular in the Victorian period when men needed to protect their waxed moustaches. The inscription says 'For the festival of Pesach' and it was probably added after purchase rather than incorporated into the original design.

puddings

Winter compôte

Serves 6

225g (8oz) each dried stoneless prunes, dried apricots, dried pears, dried apples

2 lemons, sliced

50g (2oz) each raisins, sultanas and flaked almonds

3 large pinches each of ground cinnamon and ground nutmeg

1 tablespoon brandy (optional)

600ml (1 pint) freshly squeezed orange juice

Dried fruits have always been popular in the Jewish kitchen. Dates, figs and grapes have been dried in the Middle-Eastern sun since the earliest times and the techniques were adapted to local fruits wherever Jews settled. During the cold winter months, some alcohol was added to keep out the chill: in Poland it was plum brandy, in Italy grappa and in the UK (as in France) it was more likely to be brandy.

This is a perfect dessert for the Kosher kitchen as it can be eaten at any time of the day, with meat or fish meals, and, of course, can be cooked on Friday to be used on the Sabbath. When it is not eaten before or after meat, crème fraîche is an ideal accompaniment, into which you stir 75ml (3fl oz) orange juice and 1 tablespoon brandy (optional).

Method Preheat the oven to 180°C/350°F/gas mark 4. Mix together the dried prunes, apricots, pears and apples and put half in the base of a large casserole dish. Cover with half the lemon slices. Mix together the raisins, sultanas and almonds and sprinkle half on the lemon layer. Repeat layers, using the remaining fruit and nuts. Sprinkle with the cinnamon and nutmeg.

Mix together the brandy, if using, and the orange juice and pour over the dish. Bake for 20 minutes.

Health note Although even biblical Jews understood that dried fruits were healthy, they couldn't have imagined the enormous protective value of this compôte. Each portion provides an entire day's dose of ORAC units (see page 13), which protect against ageing, cell damage, cancers and even wrinkles. Vitamins, minerals and instant energy from the fruit sugars abound, and there's even a little protein and vitamin E from the almonds. Not even my mother would have understood the mood-enhancing benefits of nutmeg or the antibacterial properties of cinnamon – but there was always a bowl of this winter dessert in our fridge.

Matzo fritters with rosewater syrup

Serves 4-6

110g (4oz) caster sugar

4 tablespoons runny honey

Juice and grated zest of 1 lemon

125ml (4fl oz) rosewater

4 eggs

6 tablespoons medium matzo meal

About 400ml (14fl oz) rapeseed or
*   sunflower oil*

Passover is a wonderful time of the year. I still remember the excitement of all the preparation, the hours spent watching my mother and her sisters creating all the special cakes and biscuits made with strange (to a child, at least) ingredients such as potato flour, ground almonds and coconut, and the disasters caused by banging any door in the house while the special Passover cake, *plaver*, was in the oven. It all culminated on the evening before Passover in the search for *chametz* – bread and cakes.

During Passover, no leavened bread must be eaten, and nothing containing even a trace of leaven is allowed to remain in the house. So, armed with a candle and a feather, my mother would search the nooks and crannies of the kitchen so that any minute crumbs could be swept up and ceremoniously burned. For the next seven days, only unleavened bread – called *matzo*, 'the bread of affliction', eaten by the Jews when they escaped from Egypt as there was no time to let the dough rise – was allowed.

At least today you can find wholemeal matzo, which makes life a little easier as many people find normal matzo constipating. There are many recipes for cooking with matzo. Here's my favourite, with the exotic Ottoman flavour of rosewater.

Method Put the sugar, honey and 3 tablespoons lemon juice into a pan with 200ml (7fl oz) water. Bring to the boil, stirring, until the sugar and honey are dissolved. Add the rosewater and set aside but keep warm.

Separate the eggs and whisk the whites until stiff. In another bowl, beat the yolks gently with the lemon zest and fold into the whites. Sift over the matzo meal, then mix thoroughly.

Heat the oil in a large, wide frying pan. Drop in the fritter mixture a tablespoon at a time and shallow-fry, turning once, until golden; you'll have to do this in batches. As you're cooking, drain each batch of fritters on kitchen paper and keep warm. Arrange the warm fritters on a serving dish and pour the rosewater syrup over them.

Baked apples stuffed with figs

Serves 4

4 large dessert apples

8 dried figs, chopped

150ml (1/4 pint) apple juice

1 tablespoon runny honey

25g (1oz) unsalted butter

There is certainly no sin in eating these apples and, combined in this popular Jewish dessert with all the traditional health-giving benefits of figs, they are delicious served with sorbet or Kosher non-dairy ice cream.

Method Preheat the oven to 200°C/400°F/gas mark 6. Cut a slice off the base of the apples so that they stand upright. Remove the cores with an apple corer. Cut 1cm (1/2in) off the end of each core and replace in the apples to form a plug.

Cover the figs with boiling water and leave to stand for 5 minutes. Drain, reserving the liquid. Pack the figs into the apples and put them into a roasting tin. Mix together the fig liquid, apple juice, honey and butter and pour over the apples. Cover the tin with foil and bake for 20 minutes.

Remove the foil and bake for a further 15 minutes.

Health note Apples are rich in pectin, a form of soluble fibre that helps reduce cholesterol, whilst figs contain anti-cancer agents, healing enzymes and digestion-improving natural chemicals.

Soya rice pudding with brazil nut compôte

Serves 6

75g (3oz) pudding (short-grain) rice

400ml (14fl oz) soya milk

4 cardamom seeds, smashed with a rolling pin

About 50g (2oz) unsalted butter

50g (2oz) Brazil nuts, ground

1 tablespoon runny honey

2 tablespoons freshly squeezed orange juice

Neither rice, soya milk nor Brazil nuts were around at the beginning of Jewish history, but Jewish cooks are nothing if not inventive and adventurous. Soya milk is an excellent alternative to cow's milk and can be used in many milk-based recipes which can't normally be eaten as part of, or soon after, a meat meal.

That can't be done, however, with this recipe because of its use of butter, which is what makes rice pudding so delicious. From a health point of view, I'm not an admirer of any margarine, but considering the great health benefits of this dessert, substituting a little Kosher margarine would be acceptable if you wanted to serve this after a meat meal.

Mixing nuts, honey and cardamoms is a traditional feature of Sephardic cooking, but this is a universal recipe we created for this book.

Method Preheat the oven to 150°C/300°F/gas mark 2. Put the rice, soya milk and cardamoms into a large pie dish greased with a little butter. Dot with the remainder of the butter. Bake for about 1 1/2 hours.

Mix together the Brazil nuts, honey and juice. Serve each bowl of rice with a spoonful of nut compote on top.

Opposite: Baked apples stuffed with figs

Pears in blackcurrant sauce

Serves 4-6

*A tiny amount of unsalted butter
(or rapeseed or sunflower oil if
you don't mix dairy and meat
products and want to eat this
after a meat meal)*

4 Conference pears, cut in half

Juice of 1 lemon

2 tablespoons brown caster sugar

*450g (1lb) blackcurrants, fresh or
defrosted, frozen*

1 tablespoon runny honey

1/2 standard glass sweet white wine

In some eastern European Jewish communities, particularly in Poland and Hungary, mixing fruit and wine made some of the most popular desserts. Here, the last of the season's fresh currants combine with the first of the autumn pears. The contrast of the sharp and sweet flavours makes a delicious end to a healthy meal.

Method Preheat the oven to 180˚C/350˚F/gas mark 4. Using as little butter as possible, grease an ovenproof dish large enough to take the pears in one layer. Place the pears in the dish, cut side down. Pour on the lemon juice and add enough water to come halfway up the sides of the fruit. Sprinkle with the sugar. Cover and bake until the pears are just tender. Drain and return to the dish.

While the pears cook, put the blackcurrants, honey and wine into a blender and whizz until smooth. (For an extra-smooth sauce, you may want to pass it through a sieve.) Pour the mixture evenly over the drained pears, cover and bake for a further 20 minutes. Chill before serving.

Health note Currants are the richest source of vitamin C and antioxidants and the pears provide the valuable fibre known as pectin.

Blackberry and apple crisp

Serves 6

*450g (1lb) tart dessert apples
(like Granny Smith)*

*450g (1lb) blackberries (fresh are
best, but defrosted frozen fruit
will work)*

2 teaspoons brown caster sugar

175g (6oz) ground almonds

175g (6oz) porridge oats

2 tablespoons runny honey

3 tablespoons flaked almonds

*75g (3oz) unsalted butter, finely
diced*

Oats weren't around in biblical times, although the wild oat was probably the source of the early cultivated oats in central Europe. The most successful species weren't widely used until the end of the 18th century, when they became popular in the poorest communities of Europe and the UK. Oats also found a ready home in the cooking of most Ashkenazi Jews, and today they are often used in biscuits, mixed with other flours to make bread and pancakes and eaten as breakfast cereals.

Thick Greek live natural yogurt makes a good accompaniment.

Method Preheat oven to 200°C/400°F/gas mark 6. Peel, core and slice the apples. Put into a lightly buttered baking dish and scatter with the blackberries. Sprinkle with the sugar and add 2 tablespoons water.

Mix together the ground almonds and oats and sprinkle over the fruit. Drizzle with the honey, scatter over the flaked almonds and dot with the butter. Bake for 30 minutes.

Health note Comparatively low in saturated fats and immensely rich in vitamins, minerals, the best sort of fibre and protective antioxidants, this is a pudding to be enjoyed at all times of the year, but the apples, honey and almonds make it a healthy alternative to a traditional autumn fruit crumble.

Olive fig tart

Serves 4-6

For the olive-oil pastry
225g (8oz) plain flour
200ml (7fl oz) olive oil
1 egg, beaten
1 teaspoon brown caster sugar

For the filling
12 fresh, ripe figs
50ml (2fl oz) double cream
100g (3½oz) live natural yogurt
1 teaspoon almond essence
2 tablespoons runny honey

What could be more biblical than this combination which includes oil from olives, figs and honey? The Old Testament abounds with mentions of all three, and the fig tree is a powerful image in Judaism: from the leaves that clothed Adam and Eve to the times of happiness and prosperity, safety and security represented by the biblical description of living under one's own fig tree.

Figs are among the most abundant fruits in the Middle East and in southern Europe. They are widely used in the cooking of orthodox Jews in Greece, Italy and Turkey, and they were extremely popular with the Sephardim, who usually finished their meals with fruit. Sacred to Hindus, Buddhists and the ancient Greeks and Romans, figs were regarded as both food and medicine.

Method To make the pastry, put all the pastry ingredients into a food-processor and blend, using the kneading blade, until they make a dough – about 2 minutes. Mould into a ball, wrap in clingfilm and leave in the fridge for at least 1 hour.

Preheat the oven to 180°C/350°F/gas mark 4. Lightly grease a 23cm (9in) loose-bottomed flan tin. Use the pastry to line the tin, and prick lightly with a fork all over. Line the pastry with non-stick baking paper, cover with dried beans and bake for 10-15 minutes. Remove the beans and paper and bake for 5 more minutes to crisp the pastry.

Cut the figs in half lengthways and arrange on the pastry. Whisk together the cream, yogurt, almond essence and honey. Pour over the figs and bake for 50 minutes, until the cream mixture is set. Serve warm or cold but not chilled.

Health note With no saturated fat, the health-giving benefits of olive oil, calcium from the yogurt and the unique cancer-protective chemicals and enzymes in figs, this is a great dessert, which actually improves digestion after a meal rather than lying heavily on the stomach.

Cinnamon-baked plums with orange mascarpone sauce

Serves 6

Unsalted butter, for greasing

*12 Victoria plums, halved and
    stoned*

*About 250ml (9fl oz) full-bodied
    red wine*

3 cinnamon sticks

2 tablespoons brown caster sugar

*75ml (3fl oz) freshly squeezed
    orange juice*

200g (7oz) mascarpone cheese

*1 large sprig (about 12 leaves) of
    mint, leaves roughly torn*

This succulent pudding came originally from a Jewish friend who lives in the Agen region of France, where it is made with the unique prune plums, *pruneaux d'Agen*, before they're dried to make the best prunes in the world. Victoria plums were the best alternative we could find, and the result is a light, delicately flavoured and healthy dessert – the perfect end to any meal.

Method Preheat the oven to 200°C/400°F/gas mark 6. Generously butter a large pie dish and lay the plums, cut side down, on top. Pour on the wine, add the cinnamon and scatter with the sugar. Cover with foil and bake until the plums are soft – about 25 minutes.

Gently mix the orange juice and mascarpone together. Serve with the mint leaves scattered over the plums and the mascarpone sauce on the side.

Health note The red wine brings cardio-protective benefits and there is lots of potassium from the plums as well as a little vitamin E and an abundance of protective antioxidants to help fight ageing. With extra protein and calcium from the mascarpone and the digestive properties of mint, this is a fighting-fit dessert.

Stuffed prunes with coconut sauce

Serves 4

250ml (9fl oz) red wine

1 tablespoon runny honey

16 stoneless ready-to-eat prunes

16 whole almonds, shelled

150ml (1/4 pint) coconut milk

Every Jewish comedian will have at least one joke in his repertoire about constipation and the popularity of prunes in Ashkenazi cooking. While there's no doubt that prunes can have a laxative effect, this is greatly over-estimated as you need to eat around twelve of these highly nutritious dried fruits at one sitting for this to happen.

Method Put the wine into a wide-bottomed pan, add the honey and heat, stirring constantly, until dissolved.

Make a lengthways cut halfway through each prune and insert an almond into each cavity, pressing the sides of the prune gently to close. Place carefully in the wine mixture, in a single layer. Bring the wine to the boil and simmer for 15 minutes. Remove the prunes and place in a serving dish.

Boil the wine until slightly reduced. Add the coconut milk and heat gently. Pour over the prunes to serve.

Health note Prunes are exceptionally rich in potassium, fibre and, above all, protective antioxidants. In fact, weight for weight, they have the highest ORAC score (see page 13) of all foods. Extra protein and vitamins from the almonds and the aromatic essence of coconut milk make this dish extremely healthy as well as delicious.

Opposite: *Cinnamon-baked plums
with orange mascarpone sauce*

Cherry clafoutis

Clafoutis started life as a speciality in France, where it was most popular in the Limousin region. With the Jewish love of sweet fruits combined with cake, it soon became a favourite among French Jews, who rapidly took it to other parts of Europe.

Serves 4

About 50 (2oz) unsalted butter

500g (18oz) black cherries, stoned

1 tablespoon finely chopped lemon balm leaves

3 eggs

50g (2oz) plain wholemeal flour

400ml (14fl oz) semi-skimmed milk

Method Preheat the oven to 200°C/400°F/gas mark 6. Grease a large, shallow, ovenproof dish with a little of the butter. Put the cherries into the dish with the lemon balm.

Whisk the eggs. Melt the remainder of the butter and whisk into the eggs. Still whisking, sift in the flour, then add the milk. Pour the egg mixture over the cherries and bake until set – about 45 minutes.

Health note Black cherries are another of the dark-coloured fruits that are rich in antioxidants, and they have the added benefit of bioflavonoids, substances that specifically protect the linings of blood vessels. Adding the lemon balm not only imparts a unique flavour, but also makes this dish calming, mood-enhancing and, interestingly, will give you special protection against viral infections, particularly cold sores and other variations of herpes – a property unique to lemon balm.

Coconut bread pudding with strawberries

Serves 6-8

6 large but thin slices of panettone

450g (1lb) strawberries, hulled and
*   halved (or quartered if large)*

850ml (1¹/2 pints) coconut milk

75g (3oz) caster sugar, plus extra
*   for sprinkling*

1 tablespoon Amaretto

5 eggs, lightly beaten

Masters of 'fusion' cooking before it was even heard of, British Jews soon adopted and adapted many traditional dishes, including bread-and-butter pudding. Borrowing from the tropics, they even used coconut milk and Kosher margarine so that this dish could be eaten with a meat meal. My favourite is this Italian version cooked by a non-Jewish friend who'd lived and worked in Italy for some years. Many Jews, who of course don't celebrate Christmas, invite non-Jewish friends to enjoy a traditional, but Kosher, Christmas meal. This recipe makes a much lighter and healthier alternative to Christmas pudding.

Method Preheat the oven to 180°C/350°F/gas mark 4. Put 2 slices of the panettone into a casserole dish, cutting it to fit snugly. Scatter over half the strawberries. Top with 2 more slices of panettone, the rest of the strawberries, then the final 2 slices of panettone. Put the coconut milk into a pan with the sugar and stir over a low heat until the sugar is dissolved. Add the Amaretto. Leave to cool slightly and beat in the eggs.

Pour the mixture over the panettone and strawberries and sprinkle over the extra sugar. Bake for 45 minutes, until golden.

Ginger lemon sorbet

Serves 6

2 teaspoons ginger extract
175g (6oz) caster sugar
Juice of 2 large (or 3 smaller)
  lemons
Lavender biscuits (see page 146),
  to serve

Sorbets have long been a favourite in all Jewish communities. Because dairy ice cream cannot be eaten as part of a meat meal, fruit-based water ices are wonderful, refreshing and palate-cleansing alternatives. Particularly in the Ashkenazi societies in the UK and North America, the water ice has become a bit of a joke as it's nearly always served during elaborate banquets at weddings and Bar Mitzvahs.

Method Put the ginger extract and sugar into a saucepan with 400ml (14fl oz) cold water. Bring slowly to the boil, stirring to dissolve the sugar, and simmer for 3 minutes. Cool completely and add the lemon juice.

Put into an ice-cream or sorbet maker and follow the machine instructions. Alternatively, put into a bowl and leave in the freezer until half-frozen. Whisk until smooth and return to the freezer. Repeat the whisking and freezing routine once more.

Leave in the freezer until needed. Serve with Lavender biscuits.

Health note This sorbet is rich in vitamin C, with the added benefit of circulatory stimulation from the ginger.

Ginger soufflé

Serves 4

Olive oil, for greasing

25g (1oz) unsalted butter

25g (1oz) plain flour

50ml (2fl oz) ginger syrup (from a
jar of stem ginger), plus 4 pieces
of stem ginger, finely sliced, to
serve

100ml (3½fl oz) milk

25g (1oz) brown caster sugar

3 yolks

4 egg whites

2 pinches of ground ginger

Of all the spices, ginger is probably the best-loved in Jewish cooking. In the Sephardic tradition, it's often used in savoury dishes just as it is in the Middle East, Far East, China and India, whereas Ashkenazi cooks use it mostly in sweet dishes such as cakes, biscuits, puddings and ice cream.

Method Preheat the oven to 200°C/400°F/gas mark 6. Brush a 18cm (7in) soufflé dish with olive oil. Cut a sheet of greaseproof paper long enough to go completely round the dish and deep enough to stand 10cm (4in) taller than the rim. Grease the paper and tie around the outside of the dish, greased side facing inwards.

Melt the butter in a pan over a low heat. Gradually add the flour, stirring continuously, until combined. Mix together the ginger syrup and milk. Still stirring continuously, add the ginger syrup and milk to the flour mixture and heat gently until thickened. Remove from the heat and beat in the sugar.

Separate the eggs and beat the 3 yolks separately into the soufflé mixture. Whisk all 4 whites until stiff and fold into the soufflé with a metal spatula or spoon.

Put the dish into a roasting tin and add enough boiling water to come about 2.5cm (1in) up the side of the dish. Bake for 30 minutes until risen and golden. Remove the paper sleeve, sprinkle with the ground ginger and serve with the stem ginger slices on the side.

Health note It is stretching credibility to describe any soufflé as truly healthy, but this is about as good as they get. There's calcium and vitamins in the milk, protein, more vitamins and iron in the eggs, and the natural chemicals in the ginger provide a substantial boost to the circulatory system.

Persian fruit salad

Serves 8

3 bananas, peeled and sliced

3 oranges, peeled, segmented and
all inner skin removed

2 apples, peeled, cored and cubed

150g (5oz) stoned dates, chopped

150g (5oz) stoned prunes, chopped

150g (5oz) dried figs, chopped

200ml (7fl oz) freshly squeezed
orange juice

Juice of 1 lime

125ml (4fl oz) orange-flower water

4 tablespoons chopped almonds

Lavender biscuits (see page 146),
to serve

This is another typical Sephardic fruit recipe, which combines fresh and dried fruits. One of the most famous Indian chefs in London, Cyrus Todiwala, told me that his favourite functions are Persian weddings because of the piles of luscious fresh and dried fruits used in so many recipes. They're equally loved by Persian Muslims, Christians and Jews.

This dish was traditional on the Jewish festival of Tu B'Shvat, which occurs on the 15th day of the Jewish month of *Shvat*. In the Western calendar, this happens in January or February, which may seem a little strange, as in Hebrew the festival is called the 'New Year for Trees', but this is when trees begin to sprout in Israel. Tu B'Shvat's praise of all the biblical species of figs, dates, pomegranates, olives and grapes signifies that healthy trees bear fruit. For orthodox Jews, this festival teaches that man, too, should 'bear fruit' in the form of good deeds.

Method Put all the fruit (fresh and dried) into a large bowl. Mix together the orange and lime juice and orange-flower water, pour over the fruit and turn gently until well combined, ensuring the bananas are especially well covered with the juice: this prevents them from browning. Leave for at least 2 hours. Scatter with the chopped almonds and serve with Lavender biscuits.

Health note: Delicious, energising, nourishing and hugely protective, this is one dessert that should be eaten throughout the year.

Matzo tools

Cakes and biscuits are an intrinsic part of the Jewish culinary tradition. If you go into any Jewish house in the afternoon - except, of course, on the Sabbath - you'll smell the aroma of baking. These wonderful iron tools were almost certainly from the late 19th century and used for stamping and punching unleavened bread. Although matzo is now generally available throughout the year, it used to be made specially for Passover and there are a whole set of rules governing its production. These implements would have only been used for Passover matzo making.

biscuits and cakes

Basic biscuits

Makes about 12 biscuits

110g (4oz) unsalted butter or
Kosher margarine or
125ml (4fl oz) olive oil
110g (4oz) brown caster sugar
1 egg yolk
4 drops vanilla essence
110g (4oz) self-raising wholemeal
flour
110g (4oz) self-raising white flour

Baking lies at the heart of the Jewish kitchen as cakes and biscuits of all sorts are an integral part of social activities and religious festivals. One of the great traditions of Ashkenazi baking is *kichles* (or *kichlach*), always served with wine and other alcoholic drinks after synagogue services and all social gatherings. My mother's original recipe used white flour and butter, but over the years I was able to point her gently in the direction of healthier cooking and she ended up using a mixture of wholemeal and white flour.

There are many variations of this basic recipe. You could try sandwiching 2 biscuits together, flat side down, with low-sugar marmalade to make Jaffa cakes; adding 3 pinches of ground ginger, cinnamon or allspice to the flour; or brushing the uncooked biscuits with a little beaten egg white and sprinkling with desiccated coconut or caraway seeds.

Method Preheat the oven to 200°C/400°F/gas mark 6. Cream together the butter, margarine or oil and the sugar. Beat in the egg yolk and vanilla essence.

Sift in the flours, mix well and knead to a dough. On a floured surface, roll out to about 5mm (^{1}/4in) thick and cut into any shapes you like (for children, you could make cut-outs of their names, for example). Put onto a lightly greased baking tray and bake until golden - about 15 minutes.

Ginger hazelnut cookies

Serves 8-10

175g (6oz) brown caster sugar
225g (8oz) hazelnuts, ground
50g (2oz) walnuts, ground
1 teaspoon ground ginger
1 teaspoon ground cloves
2 large eggs, beaten
Rice flour, for dusting

Ginger originates from the warmer regions of Asia and was used as both food and medicine in China more than 5,000 years ago. The ancient Greeks and Romans used ginger, but even before then it appeared in the earliest Sanskrit writings. One of the many spices loved in the Sephardi world, it was important to Muslims as well because of its warming properties. Islamic Paradise is said to have two fountains: one with ginger, for warming, the other with camphor, for cooling.

Method Preheat the oven to 180°C/350°F/gas mark 4. Mix together the sugar, nuts and spices. Add the eggs and beat in well.

Lightly grease a baking tray and, using a tablespoon, put mounds of the mixture on it. Bake until golden - about 30 minutes. Serve cold, dusted lightly with rice flour.

Health note Popular in most of north Africa, especially Morocco, and of course widely used in Chinese cooking, ginger stimulates the circulation and is the best of all remedies for nausea and sickness. Combined here with the protein and minerals from nuts and the digestive help from cloves, this Greek Jewish recipe is not only delicious, but is also ideal to combat travel sickness and early-morning sickness in the first stages of pregnancy.

Orange-scented pinenut and sesame snaps

Serves 4-6

*50g (2oz) mixed pinenuts and
   sesame seeds*

200g (7oz) demerara sugar

50ml (2fl oz) orange-flower water

Juice of 1/2 lime

1 teaspoon ground allspice

Although this is a favourite sweet treat in Israel, the origins of sesame seeds lie in the Balkans, the Far East and India. Sesame-seed oil was also used in India, Iraq and Syria, and sesame is the main ingredient of the traditional Middle Eastern sweet *halva*.

Method   Dry-fry the pinenuts and sesame seeds until golden. Put the sugar into a saucepan with the orange-flower water, lime juice and 75ml (3fl oz) water. Stir over a gentle heat until the sugar has dissolved, then simmer until thick and golden. Add the pinenuts, sesame seeds and allspice and heat through gently for about 2 minutes. Pour onto a cold, damp surface and roll with a rolling pin until about 1cm (1/2in) thick.

Cut into bars about 2.5cm (1in) wide and 10cm (4in) long and transfer, using a spatula, to a cold, clean surface. Leave to harden before serving.

Health note   Like all confectionery, these snaps are high in sugar, so should be regarded as a treat, but even so, the minerals, mono-unsaturated fats and vitamin E content of the seeds and nuts are extremely nutritious. Sesame seeds contain valuable quantities of bone-building calcium, so they're useful for anyone who doesn't eat dairy products.

Lavender biscuits

Serves 4

50g (2oz) brown caster sugar

110g (4oz) unsalted butter

175g (6oz) self-raising 75 per cent
    wholemeal flour

2 tablespoons chopped lavender
    leaves

2 teaspoons lavender flowers,
    stripped from their stems

These aren't traditional Jewish biscuits, but they should be as they use every Jewish cook's basic biscuit method of *kichles*. They go particularly well with the rather sweet Kosher red wine produced in Israel.

This recipe works equally well with rosemary leaves – and rosemary flowers if you can get them or if you grow your own. Add 2 tablespoons freshly grated Parmesan to the flour before mixing into the dough. Essential oils in rosemary have a specific effect on the brain and improve the memory.

Method Preheat the oven to 220°C/425°F/gas mark 7. Cream together the sugar and butter. Add the flour and lavender leaves and knead into a dough. Roll out on a floured board, sprinkle with the flowers and press them into the dough with a rolling pin. Cut with a smallish pastry cutter, about 6cm (2¹/2in) in diameter, or into squares or any other shape you prefer.

Put onto a greased baking tray and bake until golden – about 10 minutes.

Health note Stress and anxiety seem to be the traditional collective problem of Jewish mothers around the world, and the addition of lavender to this recipe makes these biscuits calming, mood-enhancing and very slightly soporific.

Peanut butter squares

Serves 8-10

110g (4oz) self-raising wholemeal
    flour

110g (4oz) self-raising white flour

1 teaspoon ground ginger

3 tablespoons crunchy peanut
    butter

2 tablespoons runny honey

3 tablespoons shelled, unsalted
    peanuts

Here's a surprisingly healthy addition to your baking repertoire. Most people think of peanuts and peanut butter as being fattening and unhealthy when in fact the exact opposite is true.

Method Preheat the oven to 180°C/350°F/gas mark 4. Mix together the flours and ginger. Rub in the peanut butter until the mixture has the texture of breadcrumbs.

Warm the honey and stir well into the mixture. Knead to a dough and roll out on a floured board.

Dry-fry the peanuts and press firmly into the dough. Cut the dough into 5cm (2in) squares. Transfer to a lightly greased baking tray and bake for 20 minutes. Serve cold.

Health note Peanuts aren't only a valuable component of any weight-loss programme because they have a low glycaemic index (which means they're broken down very slowly into sugars and consequently have little effect on insulin levels), but they also help prevent diabetes. They're a rich source of mono-unsaturated fats, which help the body eliminate cholesterol, and they're rich in protein, vitamins and minerals. The combination of peanuts and wholemeal flour in this recipe also provides valuable amounts of fibre.

Opposite: *Lavender biscuits*

Cinnamon balls

Serves 4-6

3 egg whites

*1 heaped tablespoon ground
cinnamon*

150g (5oz) ground almonds

200g (7oz) brown caster sugar

Rice flour, for dusting

At the time of Passover, the total absence of bread and the resulting dependence on *matzo* were only endurable by all my young cousins and me because of the abundance of these cinnamon balls. My mother's youngest sister, Gertie, was the cinnamon-ball maker and she produced them by the tinful for the entire family.

These are perfect for anyone who's a coeliac or who suffers from wheat intolerance. They're normally dusted with icing sugar to prevent them from sticking together, but I prefer to use rice flour instead as it doesn't increase the sugar content. Ideally, these balls should be firm on the outside, but soft and succulent in the middle. Overcooked, they turn into tooth-breakers.

Method Preheat the oven to 180°C/350°F/gas mark 4.

Beat the egg whites until very stiff. Add the cinnamon, almonds and sugar and mix well. Roll the mixture into balls about the size of a large plum, set on a greased baking tray and bake until set – about 30 minutes.

Dust with the rice flour before setting aside to cool.

Health note Though high in sugar, these cinnamon balls are rich in protein, vitamin E, minerals and the antibacterial benefits of cinnamon.

Rice and cheese bake

Serves 4-6

*1 sheet (500g/18oz) defrosted
frozen puff pastry, or make
your own*

250g (9oz) cooked short-grain rice

400g (14oz) low-fat cream cheese

2 eggs, beaten

1 tablespoon demerara sugar

3 tablespoons plump sultanas

Rice pudding is one of the most popular desserts in Portugal, and this Jewish recipe from Lisbon would have been traditionally prepared with home-made curd cheese. It provides protein, calcium, iron and fibre and combines the Sephardi favourites of rice, cheese and dried fruits.

Method Preheat the oven to 180°C/350°F/gas mark 4.

Roll out the pastry and use to line a greased 28 x 20cm (11 x 8in) tart tin. Mix together the rice, cheese, eggs, sugar and sultanas. Put the mixture into the pastry case.

Bake until the pastry is golden and the filling set – about 35 minutes.

Opposite: *Cinnamon balls*

Haricot bean cake

Serves 4-6

3 large eggs

175g (6oz) brown caster sugar

*275g (10oz) haricot beans, cooked,
  rinsed, drained and left until
  completely cold*

*Juice and grated zest of 1 large
  lemon*

2 tablespoons Amaretto (optional)

3 tablespoons ground almonds

Beans have always been popular in Jewish cooking as an addition to casseroles, soups and stews, but it's only among the Sephardi community that they're used in sweet dishes, too. This Middle-Eastern cake may sound strange, but it tastes wonderful and is an interesting alternative to the usual Ashkenazi recipes baked during Pesach when no flour is allowed.

Method Preheat the oven to 180°C/350°F/gas mark 4. Separate the eggs, reserving the whites, and beat the yolks into the sugar. Mix in the beans, lemon juice and zest and Amaretto, if using.

Beat the egg whites until stiff and fold into the mixture. Pour into a greased 20cm (8in) cake tin. Bake for 1 hour.

Leave in the cake tin until completely cold before turning out. Dust with ground almonds to serve.

Pumpkin and ginger tart

Serves 6-8

175g (6oz) demerara sugar

*3 tablespoons ginger syrup (from a
  jar of stem ginger, plus 4-6
  pieces of stem ginger, finely
  chopped to make about
  6 tablespoons*

*1kg (2¼lb) pumpkin or
  squash flesh, grated*

*1 sheet (500g/18oz) defrosted
  frozen puff pastry, or make
  your own*

The influences of the Middle East and the Ottoman Empire gave the Sephardi Jews a very sweet tooth. But they also loved all the spices, especially ginger, which combines wonderfully with the already sweet taste of pumpkin. Although this is a very popular Italian Jewish recipe, I have also eaten it in South Africa, where the very mixed Jewish community is extremely fond of pumpkin. They serve it with honey and cinnamon as a vegetable with meat dishes and add a teaspoon of ground cloves to their version of this tart.

This ends up looking like a British treacle tart, but it certainly tastes better and is much more healthy.

Method Preheat the oven to 190°C/375°F/gas mark 5. Put the sugar, ginger syrup and pumpkin or squash into a saucepan and cook over a low heat, adding a little water if necessary, until you have a thick paste – about 20 minutes. Stir in the chopped ginger, heat gently for 1 minute and leave to cool completely.

Use the pastry to line a greased 28 x 20cm (11 x 8in) tart tin. Pour in the ginger and pumpkin mixture and bake for 25 minutes. Serve cold.

Date tea bread

Serves 6-8

5 lime-blossom tea bags

*250g (9oz) self-raising wholemeal
   flour*

1 egg, beaten

200g (7oz) soft brown sugar

450g (1lb) stoned dates, chopped

Dates are one of the great survival foods that have sustained wandering travellers and nomads in the deserts of the Middle East and camel trains that criss-crossed the silk routes of the ancient world. They grew in vast stretches of land throughout north Africa, Arabia and Persia. Popular cooked with meat dishes in the Middle East and Elizabethan England, they are used here to make a delicious and healthy tea bread.

There are many variations to this bread. In fact, you can use any combination of any tea and any dried fruit: for example, Earl Grey with mixed exotic fruit, peppermint with dried apples, Lapsang Souchong with prunes.

Method Soak the tea bags in 300ml (^{1}/2 pint) boiling water. Leave until cold, squeeze the tea bags and discard. Mix the tea with all the other ingredients and leave to rest, covered (but not in the fridge), for at least 6 hours.

Preheat the oven to 180°C/350°F/gas mark 4. Butter a 1.2-litre (2-pint), approximately 23 x 13 x 7cm (9 x 5 x 2^1/2in) bread tin neatly with greaseproof paper. Pour in the mixture and bake for 30 minutes. Serve when cool.

Health note Rich in energy and fibre and with large amounts of potassium, which is important for the heart and all muscle activity, dates also provide valuable iron, copper and magnesium. Using lime blossom makes this recipe calming and relaxing: perfect as an evening treat to help you sleep.

Carrot cake with coconut

Serves 6-8

2 tablespoons runny honey

150g (5oz) demerara sugar

200ml (7fl oz) olive oil

3 eggs, beaten

1 teaspoon ground cinnamon

175g (6oz) wholemeal self-raising flour

250g (9oz) carrots, grated

110g (4oz) desiccated coconut, plus 2 tablespoons to decorate (or decorate with coconut flakes if you prefer)

75g (3oz) mixed unsalted nuts, crushed

The Jewish love affair with carrots is obvious when you see how many recipes using this vegetable appear in most Jewish cookery books. The first time I ate carrot cake was in a tiny village overlooking Lake Zurich in Switzerland, where I'd gone to visit a friend's cousin. I always assumed that this delicious cake was Swiss rather than Jewish until I discovered a variety of *kugels* (cakes, sometimes called puddings) made from vegetables cooked in cake or loaf tins, which were either sweet or savoury. Traditional to European Ashkenazim and originally made mostly of potatoes, they're now made from many different and much healthier vegetables, including sweet potatoes.

This is a moist and succulent carrot cake full of health-giving and nutritious ingredients which can be eaten with meat or milk meals.

Method Preheat the oven to 180°C/350°F/gas mark 4.

Put the honey, sugar and oil into a bowl and whisk briskly until well combined. Add the eggs and cinnamon and whisk well again. Gradually sift in the flour and whisk until well combined, then stir in the husks that have collected in the sieve. Stir in the carrots, coconut and nuts. Pour into a greased 18cm (7in) cake tin and cook for about 90 minutes.

Allow to cool and serve scattered with the extra coconut.

Three-fruit almond cake

Serves 8

1 orange

1 thin-skinned pink grapefruit

1 lime

2 tablespoons lemon juice

175g (6oz) soft brown sugar

200g (7oz) ground almonds

1/2 teaspoon baking powder

5 eggs

Is this a cake or a pudding? Who knows? Who cares? It tastes fantastic and is extremely healthy. You'd be forgiven for imagining that it's a modern Israeli recipe; in fact, it comes from the Jewish community in Stellenbosch, South Africa, a country famous for its wonderful citrus fruits.

Method Put the orange, grapefruit and lime into large saucepan, cover with water and simmer for 90 minutes. Leave to cool.

Preheat the oven to 200°C/400°F/gas mark 6.

Cut the fruit in half and take out the pips. Put the fruit pieces into a blender or food-processor with the lemon juice, sugar, ground almonds, baking powder and eggs and whizz until smooth.

Put the mixture into a greased 23cm (9in) cake tin and bake for 40–50 minutes.

Health note Much of the vitamin C will be lost during cooking, but there are protective bioflavonoids in the fruit pith, antibacterial essential oils in the skins, and carotenoids in the pink grapefruit. Protein, minerals and vitamin E from the almonds, and iron and more protein from the eggs make this an extremely healthy dessert.

Honey cake (*lekach*)

Serves 6-8

8 tablespoons runny honey

2 eggs

100g (3¹/₂oz) demerara sugar

3 tablespoons olive oil

A small cup (about 150ml/5fl oz) coffee

175g (6oz) self-raising white flour

175g (6oz) self-raising wholemeal flour

¹/₂ teaspoon ground cloves

1 teaspoon ground ginger

3 tablespoons slivered almonds

There are almost as many recipes for honey cake (*lekach*) as there are Jewish cooks. Although they're all similar, communities and even individuals add their own touches to the basic recipe. Traditionally served during Rosh Hashanah, the Jewish New Year, it is eaten as a reflection of our prayers for a sweet year to come. In our house, it was something of a mixed blessing; this recipe was given to my mother by her Dutch mother-in-law, and at every New Year celebration it was a reminder of my father's parents, grandparents, his great-grandmother, brothers, sister, uncles, aunts, nieces and nephews who vanished into the Holocaust of the Second World War. Only his youngest brother and his wife (Jo and Henny) survived, thanks to the incredible bravery of a Catholic family who hid them in the cellars under their farmhouse.

Method Preheat the oven to 190°C/375°F/gas mark 5.

Warm the honey in a small pan. Beat the eggs and sugar together.

Add the oil, warmed honey and coffee to the egg mixture. Sift in the flours, cloves and ginger, add 150ml (5fl oz) warm water and beat well. Turn the mixture into a greased 23cm (9in) tin and sprinkle with the slivered almonds. Bake for 1 hour.

Health note As cakes go (and this one always does) this is pretty healthy, but not when eaten in the Dutch manner: spread thickly with butter or with a slice of the wonderful Leiden cheese, made with spicy caraway seeds.

Prune cheesecake

Serves 4-6

*1 sheet (500g/18oz) defrosted
   frozen shortcrust pastry, or make
   your own*
75g (3oz) unsalted butter
50g (2oz) caster sugar
3 small eggs, beaten
400g (14oz) curd cheese, drained
*6 large ready-to-eat prunes,
   snipped to the size of raisins*
Grated zest of 1 large lemon

Cooked cheesecake is one of the most popular recipes from German Jewish cooking, and it is one that has spread far beyond the Jewish kitchen and bakery to become universally accepted - nowhere more so than in America, where it's a national dish. I find this type of cheesecake infinitely preferable to the non-cooked versions, which are normally made with processed, cream-like cheeses, then refrigerated to make them solidify.

Many older Jewish women made their own curd cheese by hanging muslin bags of soured milk, like my mother did, on the washing line. Dairy foods such as this cake are a traditional feature of the festival of Shavuot, the sixth day of the Hebrew month of *Sivan*: May to June in the Western calendar. This celebrates both the festival of the First Fruits and the time when the Torah (the Law) was handed down by God to the Jewish people on Mount Sinai.

Method Preheat oven to 230°C/450°F/gas mark 8.

Roll out the pastry and line a greased 18cm (7in) tart tin. Prick the base several times with a fork. Line the pastry with non-stick baking paper, cover with dried beans and bake for 10-15 minutes. Remove the beans and paper and bake for 5 more minutes to crisp the pastry.

Cream together the butter and sugar and beat in the eggs and cheese. Stir in the prunes and lemon zest. Put the mixture into the pastry case.

Put into the oven at the preheated temperature, then immediately turn the heat down to 180°C/350°F/gas mark 4. Bake until the filling is set and the pastry golden - about 25 minutes.

Health note The addition of prunes instead of the more traditional raisins gives this recipe protective qualities in addition to the protein and calcium from the curd cheese.

Index

Acknowledgements   I've wanted to write this book for many years as I am passionate about Jewish food, so first I must thank Kyle Cathie for giving me this opportunity. Working with Muna Reyal has been an absolute joy, thanks to her enormous enthusiasm and creativity. Great thanks are due to Jan Baldwin for her beautiful food photography and to Vanessa Courtier for her imaginative location photos and beautiful design. I'd also like to express my gratitude to the Jewish Museum, London and curator, Jennifer Marin, for the time and trouble they took to make so much material available. Finally, yet another opportunity for Sally and me to work with our favourite and incredibly efficient editor, Jamie Ambrose.

Thanks also to The Brick Lane Beigel Bake, 159 Brick Lane, London E1 6SB; Hampstead Seafoods, 78 Hampstead High Street, London NW3; Hampstead Tea Rooms, 9 South End Road, London NW3 2PT; Panzer's, 13-19 Circus Road, London NW8; Pomona, 179 Haverstock Hill, London NW3 4QS; Sam's Fish and Chips, 68-70 Golders Green Road, London NW11 8LN; Six-13, 19 Wigmore Street, London W1U 1PH; Steimatzky Hasifria, 46 Golders Green Road, London NW11 8LL for allowing us to photograph their premises.